book *of* faith
Lenten Journey

book *of* faith
Lenten Journey

40 Days with the Lord's Prayer

Henry F. French

BOOK OF FAITH LENTEN JOURNEY
40 Days with the Lord's Prayer

For information on Book of Faith Lenten Journey online worship helps and more about Book of Faith resources, go to bookoffaith.org.

 Book of faith is an initiative of the
Evangelical Lutheran Church in America
God's work. Our hands.

Cover design: Diana Running
Interior design: Ivy Palmer Skrade

This book was typeset using Dolly and Omnes.

Library of Congress Cataloging-in-Publication Data
French, Henry F.
  Book of faith Lenten journey : 40 days with the Lord's prayer / Henry F. French.
     p. cm.
  Includes bibliographical references.
  ISBN 978-0-8066-8069-9 (alk. paper)
  1. Lord's prayer—Meditations. 2. Lent—Meditations. I. Title.

BV230.F73 2009
226.9'6077—dc22
                 2008044342

The paper used in this publication meets the minimum requirements of American National Standard for Information Sciences—Permanence of Paper for Printed Library Materials, ANSI Z329.48-1984.

Manufactured in the U.S.A.

13   12   11   10   09   2   3   4   5   6   7   8   9   10

Contents

Preface 7

Introduction 9

How to Use this Book 14

Hints on Keeping a Journal 17

Journeying with Others 18

Journey Week One 19

Journey Week Two 35

Journey Week Three 51

Journey Week Four 67

Journey Week Five 83

Journey Week Six 99

Journey Week Seven 115

Notes 125

Preface

At its churchwide assembly in 2007, the Evangelical Lutheran Church in America affirmed the centrality of the Bible to Christian life and faith while at the same time recognizing the reality of biblical illiteracy in the church. The result is the Book of Faith initiative—a five-year program with "the goal of raising to a new level this church's individual and collective engagement with the Bible and its teaching, yielding greater biblical fluency and a more profound appreciation of Lutheran principles and approaches for the use of Scripture." *Book of Faith Lenten Journey: 40 Days with the Lord's Prayer* is one of many resources being prepared to accomplish this goal.

According to the Book of Faith Initiative's Web site, www.bookoffaith.org:

> The Book of Faith initiative invites the whole church to become more fluent in the first language of faith, the language of Scripture, in order that we might live into our calling as a people renewed, enlivened, empowered and sent by the Word.
>
> The Bible is the written Word of God that creates and nurtures faith through the work of the Holy Spirit and points us to Christ, the incarnate Word and center of our faith. The Bible invites us into a relationship with God, making demands on our lives and promising us life in Christ. The Bible tells the stories of people living their faith over the centuries and, through its demands and promises, forms us as a people of faith.
>
> The language of the Bible becomes our language. It shapes how we think and speak about God, about the world, and about ourselves. We become renewed, enlivened, and empowered as the language of Scripture forms our hearts, our minds, our community conversation, and our commitments.

Book of Faith Lenten Journey: 40 Days with the Lord's Prayer is designed to engage readers during the season of Lent with the prayer Jesus taught, a prayer that "invites us into a relationship with God, making demands on our lives and promising us life in Christ." This book is designed to be used alone by individuals or together with a spiritual friend or small group. It can readily be used as a resource for the entire congregation during Lent—worship helps and sermon starters related to the book for Sundays and Wednesday evenings in Lent are available online at bookoffaith.org.

Be sure to visit the Book of Faith Web site regularly for more resources designed to bring the book of faith and the community of faith closer together.

Introduction

When asked to teach his disciples to pray, Jesus said, "Pray then in this way," and then he taught them what we have come to call the Lord's Prayer. In Matthew's telling of the prayer in the New Revised Standard Version of the Bible, it is only sixty-two words in ten lines. It has only seven petitions. It is a short prayer; yet, as Tertullian, a third-century theologian once declared, it is a summary of the whole gospel.

If Jesus' teaching can be summed up in the Lord's Prayer in only sixty-two words, then some interpretation is in order. There is a lot of meaning packed into these ten lines, and it needs to be unpacked if the prayer is to be our road-map on the journey into a deeper relationship with God through Christ. If we are to follow Jesus in the way of God, we need to know what Jesus thought about the way of God—and it is all condensed in the ancient but ever new words that Jesus taught his followers to pray.

Many if not most of us, however, have prayed this prayer for so long and so many times that we no longer think about the words—we just say them. But rote repetition of the prayer is not praying. This, as we will discover over the next forty days, is a radical prayer, a prayer that turns things upside down. It is risky to pray such a prayer without knowing exactly what it is you are praying for.

So, how do we discover what we are praying for each time we open our mouths to say: "Our Father in heaven, hallowed be your name . . ."? In this little book, we will follow some tried and true Lutheran methods for getting to the heart of what God has to say to us in the words of the Bible.

For a broader treatment of what follows, I recommend that you get a copy of *Opening the Book of Faith: Lutheran Insights for Bible Study* and read the excellent article by Mark Allan Powell, "How Can Lutheran Insights Open Up the Bible?"[1]

Lutheran insights

LAW AND GOSPEL

As we work our way through the Lord's Prayer, we are going to ask how the text can be experienced as both law and gospel.

> Lutherans say that the Word of God speaks both law and gospel and that both must be held together for God's Word to be fulfilled. One way to describe these important terms is:
> - the *law* is that which accuses and judges us;
> - the *gospel* is that which comforts and saves us.[2]

As we read through the Lord's Prayer, we will experience ourselves being accused and judged; we will also experience ourselves being forgiven, comforted, saved. It all depends on the day, on the context within which we read, on what's going on in our life of faith. The same text may be heard as law or gospel. Today we may hear it one way, tomorrow a different way. The person next to us may hear it in a different way than we hear it. For example, "Our Father" may be a comforting word of grace to us or someone else when the loving faithfulness of God breaks upon us. It may, however, be a discomforting word of judgment when we recognize how little we act (and how little we want to act!) like trusting, obedient children of such a loving Father. The distinction between law and gospel will help us to unpack the meaning of the Lord's Prayer as we experience within it both God's word of judgment and God's words of grace, forgiveness, and salvation.

WHAT SHOWS FORTH CHRIST

Lutherans believe that the Bible discloses the reality and truth of Jesus Christ to us. We read the Bible because we want to learn about Jesus—what he said and what he did, who he was and why it matters. The Lord's Prayer is packed with such things. As we spend forty days with Jesus' prayer, we will expect to learn such things, and so find ourselves better equipped to follow him in the way of God. In the Gospel of John, Jesus prayed for his disciples, saying, "And this is eternal life, that they may know you, the only true God, and Jesus Christ whom you have sent" (John 17:3). That's why we read the Bible (and why we are study-ing the Lord's Prayer)—to know God and Jesus Christ, and thus to experience an eternal life, which begins now and continues in eternity.

SCRIPTURE INTERPRETS SCRIPTURE

There are many passages in scripture that are fairly easy to understand and oth-ers that are rather difficult.

> Lutherans believe that difficult passages of scripture are to be interpreted in light of those passages that are more readily understandable, and that all of scripture is to be interpreted in light of the Bible's central themes and motifs.[3]

The Lord's Prayer is packed with words that represent the Bible's central themes and motifs—the name of God, the kingdom of God, the will of God, the provision of "bread," forgiveness, rescue, and deliverance. As we move through the prayer, we will use other passages of scripture to help unpack these themes. You will notice many biblical references in the daily readings; follow those back to the pages of the Bible and ask yourself how they help to interpret the Lord's Prayer.

THE PLAIN MEANING OF THE TEXT

It can be awfully tempting to read meanings into a biblical text that just don't seem to be there. This can be (1) a ploy to avoid what God is saying to us in the text, or (2) a ploy to substitute what we want to say for what God is saying. In either case we have left a conversation with God's Word and are talking only to ourselves.

Lutherans have always believed that the plain meaning of the text—what it actually says, and how it was understood by the people who heard it first—is critical to understanding what it means in our context. This requires some work because it is not easy to hear in the twenty-first century how a text was heard in the first century. In this little book on the Lord's Prayer, most of that work has been done for you. In the years ahead, however, as you continue to engage God's Word in conversation, I encourage you to read Bible commentaries (especially social science commentaries), Bible dictionaries, Jesus studies, histories, and the like. There are many written for laypeople that will fine tune your ear for hearing how the Bible was heard by those who heard it first—a strong clue as to how it should be heard by us.

PUBLIC INTERPRETATION

Our book of faith—the Bible—is a public, not a private, document. That means that the interpretation of the Bible is also public and any personal understanding or application of the Bible must be done in light of what the Bible has come to mean in the larger community of faith. For this reason, you are encouraged to take this Lenten journey with the Lord's Prayer in a small group or with a spiritual friend—and you are encouraged to talk about your developing understanding of the Lord's Prayer with others in your community of faith. Lutherans try to follow Paul's advice: "Let the word of Christ dwell in you richly; teach and admonish one another in all wisdom" (Colossians 3:16).

LUTHERANS READ THE BIBLE WITH EXPECTANCY

In the pages of God's Word we expect to find both what God wants for us and what God wants from us (and we are delighted to discover that what God wants for us is precisely what God wants from us!). We expect to be challenged—and we are. We expect to be comforted, graced, empowered, saved—and we are. We expect to be judged—and we are. We expect to be forgiven and are delighted to discover that God's forgiveness goes far beyond our expectations.

A word about method

There are many ways to read the Bible. For example, it can be read devotionally, it can be read historically, it can be read as literature, it can be read in the light of Lutheran theology.[4] This book is essentially a devotional reading of the Lord's Prayer. The questions and journaling suggestions that accompany each day's readings are designed to help you enter the Lord's Prayer devotionally and meditate on its meaning for your own life of faith as well as for the life of your faith community.

The daily meditations along with the questions and journaling suggestions make this a fairly directed devotional experience. For those who have not spent much time in developing the habits and skills of devotional reading, the direction provided here should prove helpful. As you continue to open the Bible in the future, however, I encourage you to just sit with the Bible, pray for the Spirit's guidance, begin to read, and ask questions of the text that come from your own life and experience.

May your Lenten journey with the Lord's Prayer be an adventure that leads you to Easter and beyond in the grace of God.

Henry F. French

How to Use this Book

Your forty-day Lenten journey with the Lord's Prayer gives you an opportunity to learn from Jesus what it means to follow him in the way of God. It is an invitation to ponder what God has to say to us in the teaching and example of Jesus, an invitation to learn, and—in the grace of God—to live what you learn.

You will probably benefit most by fixing a special time of day in which to spend time with this book and your Bible. It is easier—especially in the beginning—to maintain a spiritual practice if you do it regularly at the same time. For many people mornings, while the house is still quiet and before the busyness of the day begins, is a good time. Others will find that the noon hour or before bedtime serves well. We are all unique. Some of us are "morning people" and some of us are not. Do whatever works *for you* to maintain a regular, daily encounter with the Lord's Prayer.

You will note that there are no readings for Sunday. The forty days of Lent traditionally exclude Sundays, the day we celebrate the resurrection of Christ.

Although this book is designed to be used during the forty days of Lent, it can be used at any time of the year. If you pick some time other than Lent for your journey with the Lord's prayer, it would still be best if you complete the journey in forty days. A deepening focus and intensity of experience will be the result. However, it is certainly better to complete the journey than to give it up because you can't get it done in forty days. Indeed, making it a forty- or twenty-week journey may better fit your schedule, and it just might be that spending a whole week, or perhaps half a week, rather than a day, reflecting on each reading, the scripture, and the prayers, and then practicing what you are learning, could be a powerfully transforming experience as well. Set a schedule that works for you, only be consistent. I suggest that you buy a notebook and, as you work your way through this book, take notes. Jot down questions and insights, new ideas, and suggestions for changes in your life of faith that occur to you.

Each day of the journey begins with a brief meditation on one of the petitions in the Lord's Prayer. The meditations tend to build on each other as they introduce you to the key ideas in Jesus' prayer. They are meant to be suggestive, not exhaustive, to stimulate your own thinking and meditation. Read slowly, letting the words sink into your consciousness. You may want to read each meditation two or three times before moving on, perhaps reading it out loud once.

Following the daily meditation, you will find the heading Biblical Wisdom and a brief passage from the Bible that relates directly to the meditation. Read the biblical text slowly (with your notebook at hand), letting the words sink into your consciousness.

After the biblical reading, you will find the heading Theological Thoughts. These are brief nuggets of insight from other biblical scholars and theologians that I have chosen to help focus the theme of the day.

Next comes the heading Silence for Meditation. Here you should spend anywhere from five to twenty minutes meditating on the readings. Begin by getting centered. Sit with your back straight, eyes closed, hands folded in your lap, and breathe slowly and deeply. Remember that breath is a gift of God, the gift of life. Do nothing for two or three minutes other than simply observe your breath. Focus your awareness on the end of your nose. Feel the breath (life) enter through your nostrils and leave through your nostrils.

Once you feel your mind and spirit settling down, open your eyes and read the daily meditation, the biblical text, and the theological nugget again. Read them slowly, focus on each word or phrase, savor them, explore possible meanings and implications. As you meditate on these readings, jot down any insights that occur to you. Do the readings raise any questions for you? Write them down. Do the readings suggest anything you should do? Write it down.

Stay at it as long as it feels useful. When your mind is ready to move on, close your eyes and observe your breath for a minute or so, offer a prayer thanking God for the gift of life and the gift of God's Word, and then return to the book.

The next heading is Questions to Ponder. Here you will find a few pointed questions on the day's readings. These are *general* questions intended for all spiritual seekers and faith communities. Think them through and write your answers (and the implications of your answers for both your own life of faith and your community of faith) in your notebook.

Many of these Questions to Ponder are designed to remind us—as Jesus would affirm—that although spirituality is always personal, it is simultaneously relational and communal. A number of the questions, therefore, apply the relevance of the day's readings to faith communities. Just remember, a faith community may be as large as a regular organized gathering or as small as a family, or the relationship between spiritual friends. Answer the questions in the context of your particular faith community.

Then move on to the heading Psalm Fragment. Here you will find a brief verse or two from the Hebrew book of Psalms that relates to the day's readings. The Psalms have always been the mainstay of prayer in the Christian tradition and always speak to the real situations in which we find ourselves.

Reflect for a moment on the Psalm Fragment and then continue on to the heading Journal Reflections. Several suggestions for journaling are given that apply the readings to your own personal experience. It is in journaling that the "day" reaches its climax and the potential for transformative change is greatest. It would be best to buy a separate journal rather than use your notebook. For a journal you can use another spiral-bound or ring-bound notebook or one of the hardcover journal books sold in stationery stores. Below you will find some suggestions for how to keep a journal. For now, let's go back to the daily format.

The Questions to Ponder and Journal Reflections exercises are meant to assist you in reflecting on the daily readings and scripture quotations. Do not feel that you have to answer every question. You may choose which questions or exercises are most helpful to you. Sometimes a perfectly appropriate response to a question is "I don't know" or "I'm not sure what I think about that." The important thing is to record your own thoughts and questions.

After Journal Reflections, you will find one more heading (two on Saturdays). In Worship Hints for Tomorrow, on Saturdays, you will find some suggestions drawn from our study of the Lord's Prayer that will help you see the implications of the prayer for Sunday worship. The last heading is Prayer for Today, a one- or two-line prayer to end your session and to be prayed from time to time throughout the day.

Hints on Keeping a Journal

A journal is a very helpful tool.[5] Keeping a journal is a form of meditation, a profound way of getting to know yourself—and God—more deeply. Although you could read *Book of Faith Lenten Journey* and simply reflect on it "in your head," writing can help you focus your thoughts, clarify your thinking, and keep a record of your insights, questions, and prayers. Writing is generative: it enables you to have thoughts you would not otherwise have had.

A few hints for journaling

1. Write in your journal with grace. Don't get stuck in trying to do it perfectly. Just write freely. Don't worry about literary style, spelling, or grammar. Your goal is simply to generate thoughts pertinent to your own life and get them down on paper.
2. You may want to begin and end your journaling with prayer. Ask for the guidance and wisdom of the Spirit (and thank God for that guidance and wisdom when you are done).
3. If your journaling takes you in directions that go beyond the journaling questions in this book, go there. Let the questions encourage, not limit, your writing.
4. Respond honestly. Don't write what you think you're supposed to believe. Write down what you really do believe, in so far as you can identify that. If you don't know, or are not sure, or if you have questions, record those. Questions are often openings to spiritual growth.
5. Carry this book, your notebook, and journal around with you every day during your journey (only keep them safe from prying eyes). Your Lenten journey with the Lord's Prayer is an intense experience that doesn't stop when you close the book. Your mind and heart and spirit will be engaged all day, and it will be helpful to have your book, notebook, and journal handy to take notes or make new entries as they occur to you.

Journeying with Others

You can use this book (and I hope you do) with another person, a spiritual friend or partner, or with a small group. It would be best for each person to first do his or her own reading, reflection, and writing in solitude. Then when you come together, share the insights you have gained from your time alone. Your discussion will probably focus on the Questions to Ponder; however, if you are working through the book with people you trust, you may feel comfortable sharing some of what you have written in your journal. No one, however, should ever be pressured to share anything in their journal if they are not comfortable doing so. It should also be a ground rule that whatever gets said in a small group stays in the group. A commitment to confidentiality will help everyone risk openness in this journey with Jesus' prayer.

Remember that your goal is to learn from one another, not to argue, nor to prove that you are right and the other person wrong. Just practice listening and trying to understand why your partner, friend, or colleague thinks as he or she does.

As those in your group all work to translate insight into action, sharing your experiences with each other is a way of encouraging and guiding each other, and provides the opportunity to provide feedback to each other—gently—if that becomes necessary.

Practicing intercessory prayer together, you will find, will strengthen the spiritual bonds of those who take the journey together. I would encourage you to spend a few moments sharing prayer requests around the theme of the day and then praying for each other and your faith community before you bring your time together to a close.

Journey Week One

Day 1—Ash Wednesday
Lord, teach us to pray.
Pray then in this way . . .

Days 2–6
Our Father in heaven, hallowed be your name . . .

Journey
Day One—Ash Wednesday

> *He was praying in a certain place, and after he had finished, one of his*
> *disciples said to him, "Lord, teach us to pray."*
> Luke 11:1

> *Pray then in this way . . .* — Command -
> Matthew 6:9a

Jesus would often go off to some lonely place to pray, sometimes alone and some-times with his disciples. Clearly Jesus needed times away from the crowds who clamored for his attention—and he thought his disciples needed to get away from it all from time to time as well.

He (and they) needed time when his attention could be completely on God, on his relationship with God, time to speak and time to listen, time to rest in the love of the one who sent him into the world for love of the world. Clearly Jesus needed the encouragement, the strengthening, the empowerment that comes from encounters with God in deep, intentional times of prayer. If he needed to pray, how much more do we?

But, not only do we need to pray—many if not most of us *want* to pray. If we stop for a moment, step aside from the many distractions of our lives, and look deep within, we find a longing to connect with God. We yearn for intimacy with the divine, the holy, the one whom Jesus called "Father." And so, we too ask, "Lord, teach us to pray."

And the request is answered. Jesus responds, "Pray then in this way," and then he teaches what we call the Lord's Prayer—words repeated so often for so long that they may have lost their edge for us. Many of us have become numb to their meaning, insensitive to the radical nature of this ancient and yet modern prayer.

"Pray then in this way . . ." These are not words of friendly advice from a gentle wisdom figure encouraging us to develop our own personal piety. Rather they are words of *command* spoken to people who have been *chosen* to follow Jesus in God's mission and who have freely accepted that remarkable calling. We lose the full force and effect of this prayer if we do not hear the words "Pray then in this way" as marching orders for people *chosen* for the mission of God—the mission of bringing justice and love, forgiveness and redemption into the world's sin and suffering and death.

Biblical Wisdom

Ask, and it will be given you; search, and you will find; knock, and the door will be opened for you.
    Matthew 7:7

Theological Thoughts

The reality encompassed in the Lord's Prayer is not a pretty picture but one of heavy conflict. . . . The prayer that our Lord taught us cannot be prayed in just any way and with just any attitude. It presupposes a perception of this world's tragedy.[6]

Silence For Meditation

Questions to Ponder

· What place should the teaching of prayer have in a community of faith?
· What are some of the distractions that numb our longing for God and keep us from prayer?
· Recall what was said about law and gospel in the introduction. In what way might Jesus' command "Pray then in this way" be experienced as law? As gospel?

Psalm Fragment

As a deer longs for flowing streams,
        so my soul longs for you, O God.
    Psalm 42:1

Journal Reflections

- Write about the place and practice of prayer in your life of faith right now as you begin this journey with the Lord's Prayer.
- In what (if any) ways does today's Psalm Fragment reflect your feelings?
- In your journal, write down your goals for this forty-day journey with the Lord's Prayer.

Prayer for Today

Jesus, teach me to pray, and grant me the faith and courage not only to pray but to follow you in the way of God. Amen.

Journey
Day 2—Thursday

Our Father in heaven, hallowed be your name . . .

When reading the Bible, it is common to focus on paragraphs, whole sentences, phrases, big words. Little words often get lost in the rush to understand. That's too bad; the meaning of a long sentence often hinges on the meaning of small words—prepositions, pronouns, adjectives. It's like cooking, where the slightest dash of spice can enhance the flavor of the whole dish.

When reading the Bible in a devotional way, don't ignore the little words. Savor each word as if it were the main course. Let each word have its own moment in your consciousness, a moment to suggest associations, to evoke insights, to raise questions. Be like the prophet Jeremiah who (metaphorically, of course) declared to God, "Your words were found, and I ate them, and your words became to me a joy and the delight of my heart" (Jeremiah 15:16).

Today we want to savor one little word—*our*. *Our* is the possessive form of the pronoun *we*. It implies something in common, as in, "We went to Europe for a week but *our* flight was delayed, *our* baggage got lost, *our* accommodations were terrible, *our* food was awful, we both got sick, and *our* trip was ruined!" Two or more people with a common experience, a common possession, a common hope, a common fear, a common joy, a common sorrow. Two or more people standing in solidarity with each other. Two or more people somehow bound together. All of this is contained in the word *our*.

"Our Father . . ." If God is *our* Father, then God is not only *my* Father. We share a Father. We are part of something larger than ourselves—a family, as it were. If God is *our* Father, then *all* other people are, in a profound sense, our sisters and brothers. We belong to and are responsible for each other. You will notice that there are no first person pronouns in this prayer. In no way is the Lord's Prayer ever *my* prayer. It is always *our* prayer, and whenever we pray it our attention should turn not only to our own needs but also to the needs of others.

We never pray this prayer alone. Whenever we pray these words we stand with every other person—whether they pray this prayer or not.

Biblical Wisdom
[There is] one God and Father of all, who is above all and through all and in all.
　　Ephesians 4:6

Theological Thoughts
The Lord's Prayer is emphatically a *we* prayer, a prayer that we utter as members of the people of God rather than as isolated individuals. We pray as a community and on behalf of all humanity and, indeed, all creatures. Not a trace of individualism is in this prayer.[7]

Silence for Meditation

Questions to Ponder
- How do you generally experience the church—as a true community or as a collection of relatively "isolated individuals"? Explain.
- In what activities or programs of your faith community do you most experience a sense of commonality, connection, and true closeness with others? In what programs or activities do you feel unconnected, separate, or even isolated from others? Why the difference?

- What does the recognition that God is not just *my* Father but *our* Father imply about God's (and the church's) mission in the world?

Psalm Fragment

How very good and pleasant it is

when kindred live together in unity!

Psalm 133:1

Journal Reflections

- Write about the difference between praying "Our Father" and "My Father."
- Reread the text from Ephesians above. How does knowing that God is "above all and through all and in all" change your view of the world and other people?
- Do you agree that "whenever we pray these words we stand with every other person—whether they pray this prayer or not"? Why or why not? If true, what are the implications? *yes*

Prayer for Today

Loving God, open my eyes that I may see other people as your children—loved by you as much as I am loved by you. Amen.

Journey
Day 3—Friday

Our Father in heaven, hallowed be your name . . .

Today we focus on one of the big words—*Father*. In the Old Testament, it is not uncommon to find God referred to as the father of Israel, that is, as the God who established Israel as his own special people (for example, Deuteronomy 32:6). It is, however, somewhat unusual to find *father* used as a term of personal address to God in the way Jesus used it. Clearly Jesus' relationship with God was both interpersonal and intimate, and the wonder is that by teaching his followers this prayer, he invites us into an equally personal and intimate relationship with God.

Jesus' world was distinctly patriarchal and his religion was distinctly Jewish. Although you can find feminine images of God in the Old Testament (for example, Isaiah 66:13), if Jesus had called God "Mother" instead of "Father," I suspect no one would have taken him seriously.

But can we call God "Mother"? In our world of domestic and sexual abuse, broken homes, and absent fathers, the word *father* can have deeply negative meanings for many people, meanings that keep them from experiencing the deeply interpersonal intimacy and love that moved Jesus to call God "Father" and to teach his followers to do the same. If calling God "Mother" opens a wounded soul to the experience of divine love, then why not?

After all, God is neither male nor female, but completely transcends such gender distinctions. The words *father* and *mother* both make the point Jesus was making when he taught his followers to pray "Our Father." We are dependent upon God as a child to a parent. We are to obey God as a child obeys a parent, trusting that whatever God asks of us will be good for us. We are to respect and love God as a child respects and loves a parent, when the parental relationship is grounded in love and care for the child.

When we pray "Our Father," we address our divine parent and stand firmly within the circle of God's love and care.

Biblical Wisdom
Yet, O LORD, you are our Father;
we are the clay, and you are our potter;
we are all the work of your hand.
Isaiah 64:8

Theological Thoughts
What is intended by the analogy of the father-child relationship? It is the recognition of the plain fact that we did not put ourselves on earth but that we find ourselves here as a result of someone else's will and action. This relationship cannot be altered or terminated. Even an explicit abrogation of the relationship by the created being cannot change the facts of life.[8]

Silence for Meditation

Questions to Ponder

- Recall what was said in the introduction about reading the Bible expectantly. What might Jesus' invitation to call God "Father" lead you to expect?
- How might calling God "Father" challenge the way you experience your life and relationships?
- Are the words "Our Father" words of law or words of gospel for you? Why?

Psalm Fragment

For it was you who formed my inward parts;
*   you knit me together in my mother's womb.*
I praise you, for I am fearfully and wonderfully made.
    Psalm 139:13-14a

Journal Reflections

- Write a short meditation on what it means to you to call God "Father" or "Mother."
- Make a list of other images of God that speak to your understanding and experience of God.
- Reflect on Psalm 139 above. Write your own prayer expressing what it means to you to be a creature placed on this beautiful blue-green planet by a loving God.

Prayer for Today

Holy God, Father and Mother, thank you for the steadfastness of your love this day and every day. Amen.

Journey
Day 4—Saturday

Our Father in heaven, hallowed be your name . . .

Although Jesus invites us into a deeply personal and intimate relationship with God, he does not invite us to domesticate God, a temptation that is all too easy to fall into. A domesticated god is a tribal god, a god who serves to sanction the political, economic, social, and individual agendas of those who have essentially created a god in their own image. A domesticated god is a safe god—one who asks nothing of us that we don't want to be asked. A domesticated god is a small god, reflecting the pettiness and serving the greed and ambition of people for whom god is a tool or weapon to be wielded in self-interest.

But God is not a tribal god wedded to the particular interests of particular people—God is the creator of all that is, a transcendent God, a God to stand in awe of, a God clothed in mystery. God cannot be contained in any ideology or even theology, nor can God be manipulated by human plans and designs. And so, to prevent any attempt to house-train God, Jesus tells us to pray to "Our Father *in heaven.*"

Those words, "in heaven," insist upon the awe and wonder that is appropriate for the creature in the presence of the creator. Although God is closer to us than we are to ourselves—in God "we live and move and have our being" (Acts 17:28)—God is *in heaven.* Which is a way of saying, "Yes, God is our Father, but *do not take the relationship for granted!*" When we pray this prayer, we might do well to remember Psalm 46:10: "Be still, and know that I am God!"

The paradox of God's immanence and transcendence is most profoundly expressed in the two creation stories in Genesis. In Genesis 1, God speaks and creation is called into being. With a word, sun and moon and stars are flung into space, the oceans, the forests, the prairies are populated. With a word, men and women are created in the very image of God. Here God is completely transcendent, all powerful, wholly Other—a God *in heaven.*

In Genesis 2, however, God creates not with a word but with hands. God plants a garden, fashions Adam from the dust of the earth, and breathes the breath of life into his nostrils. God fashions all the animals as a potter works with clay, and creates a woman to be with Adam from Adam's rib. God walks through the garden in the evening breeze calling for Adam. This is a hands-on God, immanent and intimate, connected and caring. A God who can be approached. A *Father/Mother* God.

The Hebrew storytellers were wise. God is our Father—and God is in heaven.

Biblical Wisdom

For it is the God who said, "Let light shine out of darkness," who has shone in our hearts to give the light of the knowledge of the glory of God in the face of Jesus Christ.

2 Corinthians 4:6

Theological Thoughts

Precisely because the ability to call God "Father" has become so devalued today, it is imperative that we hear the early Christian community telling us that [God] is "in heaven."[9]

Silence for Meditation

Questions to Ponder

· In your faith community, in what ways is God's transcendence emphasized? God's immanence? Is it a good balance? Why or why not?
· What is lost when the sense of God's transcendence is lost? When the sense of God's immanence is lost?
· Give examples of the human attempt to domesticate God within our culture.

Psalm Fragment

When I look at your heavens, the work of your fingers,
the moon and the stars that you have established;
what are human beings that you are mindful of them,
mortals that you care for them?

Psalm 8:3-4

Journal Reflections

- Write a reflection on the ways in which you personally experience God's transcendence.
- Write a reflection on the ways in which you personally experience God's immanence.
- What does it mean to you to say that "In [God] we live and move and have our being"?

Worship Hints for Tomorrow

- Just before the congregation prays the Lord's Prayer together, in the silence of your heart ask Jesus, "Lord, teach us to pray."
- When you "pass the peace," look at each person and think to yourself, "This is my brother. This is my sister." Reflect on the experience later in the day.

Prayer for Today

Our Father in heaven, do not let me lose either the sense of awe in your transcendence or the comfort of your immanence. Amen.

Journey
Day 5—Monday

Our Father in heaven, hallowed be your name . . .

And now we come to the first of seven petitions in the Lord's Prayer—"*hallowed be your name.*" According to the form of the Greek verbs, in this petition and the two that follow, we are asking God to act in ways that God should act, and we are asking God to enable us to act in ways we should act. "God, *you* make your name holy—and enable *us* to make your name holy in all we do." "God, *you* make your righteous kingdom come—and enable *us* to be agents of your coming kingdom in all we do." "God, *you* cause your will to be done on earth as in heaven—and enable *us* to do your will as well." We are bold to ask God to act in ways that vindicate God's righteousness; we are bold to ask God to enable us to act in ways that express God's righteousness.

It takes a bit of chutzpah to do this! To remind God that the hallowing of God's name, the coming of God's kingdom, and the doing of God's will is *first* God's responsibility and *second* ours seems a bit uppity coming from the creature to the creator, the child to the Father in heaven. Perhaps that is why on Sunday, the pastor often reminds us that we should "pray with confidence in the words our Savior taught us." Our confidence and boldness come from Jesus' telling us that it's okay to speak with God in this way.

To pray these first three petitions of the Lord's Prayer is risky because it expresses our commitment to serve God's purposes, our willingness to be used by God in bringing love, justice, compassion, forgiveness, mercy, peace, and hope to our hurting and hurtful world. When we live this way, we hallow God's name. It is risky business because the forces of darkness that stand against God will stand against those who stand with God. This is not a prayer for the faint of heart. As Jesus reminds us, God's name(s) are not made holy by simply repeating them. "Not everyone who says to me, 'Lord, Lord,' will enter the kingdom of heaven, but only the one who does the will of my Father in heaven" (Matthew 7:21).

Those who pray this prayer with a deep awareness of what they are doing go to church. They hallow God's name in worship, and receive from God and each other the faith, wisdom, strength, and courage to hallow God's name out in the world where they live and work and play.

> *Biblical Wisdom*
> *Why do you call me "Lord, Lord," and do not do what I tell you?*
> Luke 6:46

> *Theological Thoughts*

[God's name is hallowed] whenever the Word of God is taught clearly and purely and we, as God's children, also live holy lives according to it. To this end help us, dear Father in heaven! However, whoever teaches and lives otherwise than the Word of God teaches profanes the name of God among us. Preserve us from this, heavenly Father![10]

Silence for Meditation

Questions to Ponder

- What changes might we expect to find in our society if God's name were truly hallowed?
- In our culture, is God's name profaned more than it is made holy? Explain.
- What evidence do you see of God's name being made holy? Of being profaned?

Psalm Fragment
Teach me to do your will,
for you are my God.
Let your good spirit lead me
on a level path.
Psalm 143:10

Journal Reflections

- In Leviticus 19:2, God tells the people, "You shall be holy, for I the LORD your God am holy." Write a short meditation on what this means to you.
- Have you ever experienced praying the Lord's Prayer as a "risky business"? Explain.
- Describe in your journal times, places, and activities when you have felt the holiness of God.

Prayer for Today

Holy God, may the way I live today, what I say and what I do, mirror your holiness. Amen.

Journey
Day 6—Tuesday

Our Father in heaven, hallowed be your name . . .

God is called by many names in the Old Testament, but they are largely descriptive rather than personal: "Marvelous," "Strong One of Jacob," "He of the Mountain," "Mighty One," "Rock," "Refuge," "King." It is interesting to read through the Old Testament and make note of the many adjectives, nouns, and images used to attempt to name that which the human mind cannot fully grasp. Given the limitations of human understanding, if God does not disclose God's name, it will not be known.

According to the book of Exodus, God did exactly that—disclosed God's name to Moses before sending him to Egypt to liberate the Hebrew slaves from captivity. When Moses asked God what to tell the Hebrews when they asked who sent him to them, God replied "Yahweh," which can be translated as I AM WHO I AM, OR I AM WHAT I AM, or I WILL BE WHAT I WILL BE, or simply, I AM (Exodus 3:13-15). It is a strange name, hardly a name at all, but one that should evoke a sense of healthy fear. It declares that God IS in a way that humans are not, and God should thus be taken with great seriousness.

In ancient Israel, the name of God was considered so holy that it was not to be spoken or written. Instead of writing *Yahweh*, the writers of the Bible wrote only the four consonants in the name, YHWH, a sign to the reader that, rather than pronounce the holy name, they should read the word as either *Adonai* (Lord) or *Elohim* (God). The convention continues today. When you read your Bible and find LORD or GOD in all capital letters, it is a sign that the Hebrew text has YHWH representing *Yahweh*, the holy name of God.

The Lord's Prayer is an invitation to ponder the sacred, to wonder about I AM, the mystery from which we came and to which we shall return.

When God disclosed God's name to Moses, God spoke from a burning bush. As Moses approached the bush, he was told to take off his shoes because the ground on which he stood was holy ground. With reference to this event, the poet Elizabeth Barrett Browning wrote: "Earth's crammed with heaven, | And every common bush afire with God: | But only he who sees, takes off his shoes, / The rest sit round it and pluck blackberries." We—especially people of Christian faith—should all be running around barefoot. Sadly, too many of us have blackberry juice running down our chins. *Our Father in heaven, hallowed be your name.*

Biblical Wisdom
I am the LORD, that is my name.
    Isaiah 42:8

Theological Thoughts
The problem with the Lord's Prayer is neither in its content nor its historicity, but its familiarity. Many congregants don't actually think of the meaning of the words or, if they do, find only comfort rather than a challenge.[11]

Silence for Meditation

Questions to Ponder
- How might a community of faith help promote a sense of the sacredness of God's name?
- It might seem strange to think that God's name is not God, it is Yahweh. Would it make any difference to you to think of God as Yahweh (I AM) instead of as "God" or "Lord"? Explain.
- The Second Commandment tells us that we are not to misuse the name of God. In what ways is the name of God commonly misused in our world?

Psalm Fragment
And those who know your name put their trust in you,
        for you, O LORD, have not forsaken those who seek you.
    Psalm 9:10

Journal Reflections
- Write a short meditation titled "Making God's Name Holy."
- Write a brief prayer to Yahweh that expresses your sense of wonder at the relationship between Yahweh and humankind.

- In your day-to-day life, do you often run around "barefoot" or more often find "blackberry juice" running down your chin? Explain.

Prayer for Today

Holy God, enable me to see that all ground is holy ground for you are always with us. Amen.

Journey Week Two

Days 7–12
Your kingdom come...

Journey
Day 7—Wednesday

Your kingdom come . . .

Now we will study for a week what we could profitably spend a year—or more! We will be thinking together about the one thing that Jesus seemed to think about most—the kingdom of God. In the Gospels, the word *kingdom* appears some 123 times; Jesus uses the word 98 times. It is at the heart of his message. Mark—the earliest of all the Gospels—records the beginning of Jesus' ministry this way: "Jesus came to Galilee, proclaiming the good news of God, and saying, 'The time is fulfilled, and the kingdom of God has come near; repent, and believe in the good news'" (Mark 1:14-15).

And the "good news," of course, is that the kingdom is for everyone. The only ones excluded are those who exclude themselves, those who—for one reason or another—do not want to live under the rule of God.[12]

Which brings us to a paradox: the kingdom both is and is not. It has begun in the life of Jesus, and it continues to spread in and through the lives of people who follow Jesus—but it has not yet come in its fullness and completeness. The world is still mostly a mess. All creation does not yet live under the rule of God. When we pray "your kingdom come," we are praying for *God* to make his rule complete, we are praying for God to clean up the mess we have made. But, we are also praying that God's kingdom would come to and through us; we are praying that we would live faithfully under God's rule, that we would be part of the clean-up team.

Even a quick reading of the Gospels is enough to show that the kingdom of God, the rule of God, is the rule of love and justice. The rule of God is the rule of compassion and mercy, the rule of forgiveness. The rule of God is the rule of equity, of dignity, of peace and prosperity for all—not for the few at the expense of the many, but for all. The rule of God, in short, is the rule of life—fullness and richness of life for everyone. That's what we ask God to make happen when we pray "your kingdom come." And we also ask for the grace to help make it happen.

Biblical Wisdom

Once Jesus was asked by the Pharisees when the kingdom of God was coming, and he answered, "The kingdom of God is not coming with things that can be observed; nor will they say, 'Look, here it is!' or 'There it is!' For, in fact, the kingdom of God is among [and within][13] *you."*

Luke 17:20-21 *Among & within are the same Greek word - can it mean both?*

Theological Thoughts

[God's kingdom comes] whenever our heavenly Father gives us his Holy Spirit, so that through his grace we believe his Holy Word and live godly lives here in time and hereafter in eternity.[14]

Silence for Meditation

Questions to Ponder

- Does it surprise you that the kingdom of God was the centerpiece of Jesus' teaching? Why or why not?
- Does it change your thinking to consider the kingdom of God as the "rule" or "reign" of God? Explain.
- What are the implications for the church in saying that "the kingdom both is and is not"?

Psalm Fragment

For the word of the LORD is upright,
and all his work is done in faithfulness.
He loves righteousness and justice;
the earth is full of the steadfast love of the LORD.
Psalm 33:4-5

Journal Reflections

- Write a short meditation on what it means to you to live under the rule of God.
- Write a short meditation describing your relationship to God at this moment.
- In what ways is "the kingdom of God . . . among [and within] you"?

Prayer for Today

God of justice, remind me today that I am living under your rule, within your kingdom. Amen.

Journey
Day 8—Thursday

Your kingdom come . . .

People are interested in power, interested in being in control, in calling the shots, in setting the agenda. People care about position and privilege. But not in the kingdom of God.

Once when Jesus' followers were worrying about divvying up the positions of power and privilege in the kingdom, Jesus set them straight by saying, "You know that the rulers of the Gentiles lord it over them, and their great ones are tyrants over them. It will not be so among you; but whoever wishes to be great among you must be your servant" (Matthew 20:25b-26). Jesus turns things upside down. That's the way it is under the rule of God.

On another occasion, his followers (who were often a bit slow to catch on) asked, "Who is the greatest in the kingdom of heaven?" His answer: "Truly I tell you, unless you change and become like children, you will never enter the kingdom of heaven. Whoever becomes humble like this child is the greatest in the kingdom of heaven" (Matthew 18:1-4).

The kingdom of God is a relationship between us and God in which we acknowledge our dependence upon God. Children are good at this. Children are very relational creatures. Indeed, nothing matters more than their relationships with parents, siblings, relatives, and others who love them and care for them—and who they love back. They don't need to acknowledge their dependence, it goes without saying, and it's not a bad thing—it is just the way the world is for them. And (in a good family) the very young live joyfully in the confidence that the "rule" of their parents is naturally good.

As children grow from toddlerhood to adulthood, however, this broken world of ours teaches them different ways of being. Power, position, and privilege become quite important—as they were to Jesus' earliest followers. Perhaps that's why Jesus' announcement of the good news of the kingdom or rule of God was accompanied by the call to repent, the call to turn around and return to the childlike faith that what God wants for us and from us is and always will be good.

Biblical Wisdom

Jesus said, "Let the little children come to me, and do not stop them; for it is to such as these that the kingdom of heaven belongs."
Matthew 19:14

Theological Thoughts

When we pray "Thy kingdom come," we are not relying on our virtue or ingenuity, or even our understanding of what we ask for, but on the power of the Holy Spirit to help us welcome God's loving interventions.[15]

Silence for Meditation

Questions to Ponder

- Why is power (the ability to control others) not a characteristic of the kingdom of God?
- When Jesus calls us to be "humble" like a child, what do you think he means by humility?
- Is Jesus' call to repent a threat or a promise (law or gospel)? Explain.

Psalm Fragment

But I have calmed and quieted my soul,
*   like a weaned child with its mother;*
*   my soul is like the weaned child that is with me.*
Psalm 131:2

Journal Reflections

- Make a list of the ways in which you exercise power over others. How do you use your power? Anything you might need to repent of?
- In what (if any) ways do your human relationships mirror your relationship with God?
- Write about the differences between "childlike" faith and "childish" faith. How would you describe your faith?

Prayer for Today

God, help me become aware of the ways in which I exercise power in my relationships and give me the grace to serve rather than be served. Amen.

Journey
Day 9—Friday

Your kingdom come...

Most of us worry a lot. We are fearful creatures, full of anxiety. There seems to be good reason. We live in a competitive if not cutthroat world, and we wonder and worry if there will be enough for us. It is hard to feel secure when financial institutions fail, when prices go up and salaries don't, when the housing market collapses, when pensions fold, when healthcare costs skyrocket, when both personal and national debt goes through the roof. Most of us worry a lot—both the well-off and the not-so-well-off. When we pray "your kingdom come," we are seeking a way out of worry, a way beyond fear.

In the Sermon on the Mount, Jesus shows a deep understanding of human anxiety. He pinpoints our many worries about what we will eat and what we will drink and what we will wear—metaphors for the many fears, anxieties, desires, cares, and distractions that constantly consume us. Then he asks a question that we would all do well to ponder: "Is not life more than food, and the body more than clothing," (Matthew 6:25-31). It is—if life is lived under the rule of God.

Rather than worry about what we will eat or drink or put on, Jesus suggests that we trust God for all that. If we did, we would discover that we need much less than we think we do to have a life that is good for us and for others. God knows what we *need*, and rather than focus on all that, we should "strive first for the kingdom of God and his righteousness, and all these things will be given to you as well" (Matthew 6:33).

In the Gospel of Luke, right after telling his followers to strive first for the kingdom, Jesus tells them: "Do not be afraid, little flock, for it is your Father's good pleasure to give you the kingdom" (Luke 12:32). Another paradox. God *gives* us the kingdom; we must *strive* for it. God gives us the kingdom. God has created the world in such a way that if everyone were satisfied with enough there would be enough for everyone. It is for us to strive for such a reality.

When we pray "your kingdom come," we pray that God would bring about equity and fairness and dignity and richness of life for everyone. And we pray that we would not take more than enough of what God provides until everyone has enough.

Biblical Wisdom

I do not mean that there should be relief for others and pressure on you, but it is a question of a fair balance between your present abundance and their need, so that their abundance may be for your need, in order that there may be a fair balance. As it is written, "The one who had much did not have too much, and the one who had little did not have too little."
    2 Corinthians 8:13-15

Theological Thoughts

Unexpectedly, quite surprisingly, politics has crept into our Christian praying at this point. Here we were, talking about God, heaven, holiness, and suddenly we find ourselves in the middle of a political argument about a kingdom, transferred to some new place that calls into question the old places in which we have lived. We have not prayed, "Lord, bless our nation," or "Lord, protect my family." We pray "*your* kingdom come."[16]

Silence for Meditation

Questions to Ponder

- Is it true that we need much less than we have to live a happy, meaningful life? Explain.
- If, as Jesus suggests, life is more than food and the body more than clothing, what is life really about?
- In what ways does your faith community both receive and strive for the kingdom of God?

Psalm Fragment

I bless the LORD who gives me counsel;

in the night also my heart instructs me.

Psalm 16:7

Journal Reflections

- Make a list of things you worry about.
- Can you imagine a life without worry or anxiety? What would have to change to relieve your worries?
- If you were to "strive first for the kingdom of God and his righteousness," what would that mean for you and how might that change things for you?

Prayer for Today

God, let me cast my worries on you, trusting you know better than I what I truly need. Amen.

Journey
Day 10–Saturday

Your kingdom come . . .

When we pray for the kingdom to come, we are, in a profound way, praying for love to come. Jesus rejected the then-popular notion that God's kingdom would come through violence against those opposed to the coming of the kingdom. At one point, he told his followers, "You have heard that it was said, 'You shall love your neighbor and hate your enemy.' But I say to you, Love your enemies and pray for those who persecute you, so that you may be children of your Father in heaven" (Matthew 5:43-45). Like Father, like child—or so it is supposed to be.

The way of God is the way of love. The early Christians seemed to know this, and their life together, while by no means perfect, demonstrated it (for example, Acts 2:44). Paul knew it. He tells us, "Owe no one anything, except to love one another" (Romans 13:8). Martin Luther knew it. He tells us, "A Christian lives not in himself but in Christ and in his neighbor. Otherwise he is not a Christian. He lives in Christ through faith, in his neighbor through love."[17]

The rule of God is the rule of love. A scribe (an expert in the law) once asked Jesus which commandment was the most important. To paraphrase his answer, Jesus replied that the first was to love God who made you and the second was to love your neighbor as yourself. The scribe agreed: "You are right, Teacher; you have truly said that 'he is one, and besides him there is no other'; and 'to love him with all the heart, and with all the understanding, and with all the strength,' and 'to love one's neighbor as oneself,'—this is much more important than all whole burnt offerings and sacrifices." To which Jesus replied, "You are not far from the kingdom of God" (Mark 12:28-34).

Not far? Why not in? Perhaps because Jesus saw a difference between knowing the right answers and living the right answers. The distance between "not far" and "in" is the distance between talking about love and loving. After all, he did tell his followers, "Not everyone who says to me, 'Lord, Lord,' will enter the kingdom of heaven, but only the one who does the will of my Father in heaven" (Matthew 7:21).

Biblical Wisdom

Little children, let us love, not in word or speech, but in truth and action.
  1 John 3:18

Theological Thoughts

Seeing the kingdom at hand necessitates a response, a decision. We call this repentance. Will we be part of this kingdom or not? In saying "your kingdom come" we are acknowledging that faith in Jesus is not simply an idea or an emotion. It is a concrete reality in which we are to become part or else appear to be out of step with the way things are now that God has come into the world in Jesus.[18]

Silence for Meditation

Questions to Ponder

- Jesus asks us to love our enemies. Why, then, is there so much physical, psychological, and spiritual violence done in the name of religion—even the Christian religion?
- What do you think Luther meant when he said, "A Christian lives not in himself but in Christ and in his neighbor. Otherwise he is not a Christian"?
- What differences do you see between understanding Christianity as a way of belief or thought and understanding Christianity as a way of life?

Psalm Fragment
I love you, O LORD, my strength.
  Psalm 18:1

Journal Reflections

- Write a short meditation on the rule of God as the rule of love.
- Write about ways in which you experience Jesus' command to love our enemies and pray for those who persecute us as law, and ways in which you experience it as gospel.
- Write a short prayer for someone you don't particularly like or someone who has hurt you in any way. What will you ask for?

Worship Hints for Tomorrow

- As you sit in the pew, slip your shoes off as a sign to yourself (and anyone who notices!) that you are aware of the holiness around you.
- After worship, perhaps over a cup of coffee, strike up a conversation with someone you don't particularly like or someone who has hurt you in any way.

Prayer for Today

God of love, today I will seek to follow the rule of love in all my relationships, trusting in your Spirit to guide my way. Amen.

Journey
Day 11—Monday

Your kingdom come...

There are many images of the kingdom of God in Jesus' teaching, but dominant among them are images of eating together, of food and drink, of growth, and of value beyond measure. In Matthew 13:31-33, 44-48, Jesus tells five short parables that give us word pictures of the way he thought about the kingdom.

First, the kingdom is like a *mustard seed*. A tiny seed is planted. It grows. It takes time, but it grows. It becomes a shrub and then at last a tree, and birds find refuge and food, a place to call home in its branches. From the planting of a tiny, seemingly insignificant, practically worthless seed, over time *shelter and safety* for others come. Such is the kingdom.

The kingdom is like *yeast*. A woman making bread mixes a small amount of yeast into the flour and it changes things. Over time the dough rises and there is bread to feed the hungry. No yeast, no bread. Such is the kingdom.

The kingdom is like *treasure* hidden in a field. A man finds it, sells all that he has, and buys the field. Nothing that we think has value and is worth striving for comes anywhere close to the value of the kingdom. It is the only treasure worthy of our striving, worthy of our prayer. Such is the kingdom.

The kingdom of God is like a *merchant* who finds a pearl of great price. He is a man who knows a good deal when he sees it. He sells all that he has and buys that pearl. With great joy and single-minded devotion he goes after that which has great value. So it is in the kingdom where men and women of faith live with great joy and single-minded devotion under the rule of God because no other life makes sense. Such is the kingdom.

The kingdom is like a *net* thrown into the sea. It catches fish of every kind. That's the net's job. Such is the kingdom—radically inclusive, drawing everyone in, good and bad together. Separating the good from the bad? That's God's job, not for us to worry about, for only God knows which is which. Such is the kingdom for whose coming we pray.

Biblical Wisdom

At daybreak [Jesus] departed and went into a deserted place. And the crowds were looking for him; and when they reached him, they wanted to prevent him from leaving them. But he said to them, "I must proclaim the good news of the kingdom of God to the other cities also; for I was sent for this purpose."
Luke 4:42-43

Theological Thoughts

If there is one single metaphor for the kingdom that stands out from all others, it is that of God's abundance, graciously offered to all in festive meals.[19]

Silence for Meditation

Questions to Ponder

- Why do you think Jesus chose ordinary things to use as symbols of the kingdom?
- Which of the images of the kingdom in today's reading speak most powerfully to you? Why?
- Jesus' images of the kingdom come from his world. What images might we use from our world to describe the kingdom?

Psalm Fragment

With my whole heart I seek you;
do not let me stray from your commandments.
I treasure your word in my heart,
so that I may not sin against you.
Psalm 119:10-11

- Write about ways in which you serve as "yeast"—a positive agent of change.
- Reflect on ways in which you may (or may not) be like the merchant who found the pearl of great price.
- In what ways might your life be a parable of the kingdom?

Prayer for Today

Lord, today I intend to be as welcoming and inclusive as a "net" of the kingdom. Amen.

Journey
Day 12—Tuesday

Your kingdom come . . .

It is terribly important that we recognize that the kingdom has broken into (and continues to break into) human reality—first in the life of Jesus and second in the lives of those who follow Jesus. But, as we mentioned on day 7, there is also a "not yet" dimension to the kingdom. Even as we live now under God's rule, we wait in hope (and pray) for the final coming of the kingdom in all its completeness.

When we think about the coming kingdom, we think of human life brought to perfection. We think about the reign of perfect justice and perfect love; we think about goodness, truth, and beauty. We think about seeing God face to face and finally knowing what is now too great for human minds to grasp. "Now we see in a mirror, dimly, but then we will see face to face. Now I know only in part; then I will know fully, even as I have been fully known" (1 Corinthians 13:12).

When we think about the coming kingdom, we are reduced to vision and poetry:

On this mountain the LORD of hosts will make for all peoples
a feast of rich food, a feast of well-aged wines,
of rich food filled with marrow, of well-aged wines strained clear.

And he will destroy on this mountain
> the shroud that is cast over all peoples,
>
> the sheet that is spread over all nations;
>
> he will swallow up death forever.

Then the Lord GOD will wipe away the tears from all faces,
> and the disgrace of his people he will take away from all the earth,
>
> for the LORD has spoken. (Isaiah 25:6-8)

It is for this we pray when we say "your kingdom come." It is the hope that sustains us as we work now under the rule of God to turn this old world "upside down" (Acts 17:6-7).

Biblical Wisdom
Then people will come from east and west, from north and south, and will eat in the kingdom of God.
> Luke 13:29

Theological Thoughts
For Jesus, the kingdom of God is at the same time both already there and has not yet arrived. It has already dawned, is already growing, but has not yet been accomplished.[20]

Silence for Meditation

Questions to Ponder

- What are the signs of the kingdom that broke into human reality in the life of Jesus?
- What signs do you see of the kingdom, breaking in through the lives of Jesus' followers?
- Which dimension of the kingdom—the "now" or the "not yet"—gets the most attention in your faith community? Explain.

Psalm Fragment
Great is the LORD and greatly to be praised
in the city of our God.
Psalm 48:1

Journal Reflections

- Write a short meditation on the feelings that the vision in today's reading evokes in you.
- Where is your focus usually? On the "now" or the "not yet" dimension of the kingdom? Explain.
- Write a short poem expressing your vision (hope) for the coming kingdom of God.

Prayer for Today

God of today and tomorrow, today and tomorrow I want my life to be a sign of your kingdom. Amen.

Journey Week Three

Days 13–18

Your will be done, on earth as in heaven.

Journey
Day 13–Wednesday

Your will be done, on earth as in heaven.

It seems important—doing the will of God. At one time Jesus told his followers, "My food is to do the will of him who sent me and to complete his work" (John 4:34). At another time, when told that his mother and brothers had come to see him, he declared, "Here are my mother and my brothers! Whoever does the will of God is my brother and sister and mother" (Mark 3:34-35). It seems that being a part of the family of God involves doing the will of God.

So what exactly is the will of God? One might point to the Ten Commandments as the will of God. One might point to all of Jesus' teaching. One might also point to Micah 6:8—the best one-line description of both the will of God and a truly Christian lifestyle that can be found in the Bible. It is a text that sums up both the Ten Commandments and Jesus' teaching:

[God] has told you, O mortal, what is good;
    and what does the LORD require of you
but to do justice, and to love kindness,
and to walk humbly with your God? (Micah 6:8)

The will of God in a nutshell.

Naïve though it may seem, one wonders how the world would change if politicians and diplomats, business leaders and economists, and all the other powers that be would ask themselves three questions before making decisions that affect the lives of countless people: What does this have to do with justice? What does this have to do with loving kindness? What does this have to do with walking with God?

Given the broken, sinful nature of humankind, it's not going to happen anytime soon. But what if these questions guided the agenda, decisions, and actions of every Christian faith community, and of each individual Christian man, woman, and child? How would the world change—given the fact that there are some two billion Christians in the world—if people who pray "your will be done" took God's will a bit more seriously? What would happen if we all were a bit more serious in taking the will of God as "a lamp to [our] feet and a light to [our] path" (Psalms 119:105)?

Biblical Wisdom
Do not be conformed to this world, but be transformed by the renewing of your minds, so that you may discern what is the will of God—what is good and acceptable and perfect.
   Romans 12:2

Theological Thoughts
In fact, God's good and gracious will comes about without our prayer, but we ask in this prayer that it may also come about in and among us.[21]

Silence for Meditation

Questions to Ponder
- At this point in our Lenten journey, what do you think it means to "do justice"?
- What do you think it means to "love kindness"?
- What do you think it means to "walk humbly with your God"?

Psalm Fragment
He leads the humble in what is right,
        and teaches the humble his way.
   Psalm 25:9

Journal Reflections
- Reflect on the degree to which the will of God is a lamp to your feet and a light to your path.
- Write a short meditation on how you personally "walk humbly with your God."

- Are there any spiritual practices you want to learn that might help you in your walk?

Prayer for Today

Jesus, you are the light of the world, and you have declared your followers to be the light of the world. Let it be so. Amen.

Journey
Day 14–Thursday

Your will be done, on earth as in heaven.

Today, and for the next two days, we will take a closer look at God's will through the lens of Micah 6:8 (see yesterday's reading). Jesus' own teaching was right in line with Micah 6:8. For example, at one point he sharply criticized some religious people of his day who were fastidious about observing religious rules and rituals while they "neglected the weightier matters of the law: justice and mercy and faith" (Matthew 23:23). Sounds a lot like justice, kindness, and walking with God.

The demand for justice in the Bible is grounded in the nature of God. God is just; it is God's will that we be just (for example, Deuteronomy 10:18-19). And as the prophets and Jesus make clear, justice is not a question (as we often mistakenly believe) of civil or criminal law—it is about equity, fairness, sharing the abundance that God has so graciously provided. As we hinted at on day nine of this forty-day journey, in a truly just world (one living under the rule of God), nobody would have more than enough of the material necessities of life until everyone had enough. Then it would be all right to have more than enough—but only then. As folks who live in a society that has been diagnosed as suffering from "affluenza,"[22] we would do well to ponder God's will for justice.

Justice for the oppressed means deliverance; for the oppressor it means judgment. Justice overturns the gross political, economic, and social inequities that diminish, damage, or even destroy the lives of some for the benefit of others. This matters to God; it mattered to Jesus; it therefore matters to those who follow Jesus.

Both Matthew and Luke declare that the Spirit of God anointed Jesus to "proclaim justice" and bring "justice to victory" (Matthew 12:18-21; Luke 4:16-21). It's what he was about. It is what we are to be about. It is why we pray, "Your will (not my will) be done on earth."

Biblical Wisdom
Wash yourselves; make yourselves clean;
    remove the evil of your doings
    from before my eyes;
cease to do evil,
    learn to do good;
seek justice,
    rescue the oppressed,
defend the orphan,
    plead for the widow.
  Isaiah 1:16-17

Theological Thoughts
"Your will be done on earth as in heaven" is first a declaration of what God is doing before it implies anything that we ought to do.[23]

Silence for Meditation

Questions to Ponder
- Jesus gives priority to doing justice over observing religious rules and rituals. Do you think that religious rules and rituals might be used to mask injustice? Explain.
- Is it possible for something to be legal and yet unjust? Explain.
- Do you agree that American society suffers from "affluenza"? Why or why not?

Psalm Fragment
O LORD, you will hear the desire of the meek;
    you will strengthen their heart, you will incline your ear

to do justice for the orphan and the oppressed,
    so that those from earth may strike terror no more.
    Psalm 10:17-18

Journal Reflections

- Write a short meditation on ways in which you identify with people treated unjustly.
- Make a list of the forms of injustice you have witnessed in the world.
- Make a list of the forms of justice you have witnessed in the world. (Compare the lists. Any conclusions?)

Prayer for Today

Loving God, today, in the decisions I make that get me from morning to night, may I seek to be fair in my dealings with others. Amen.

Journey
Day 15—Friday

Your will be done, on earth as in heaven.

At first glance, it may seem somewhat strange to hear that God wills us to love kindness. In our impersonal, high-powered, high-pressured, high-tech, high-maintenance world, it seems that there should be more productive, more efficient, certainly more important items on God's agenda. At second glance, maybe kindness is just what we need to make the world more humane.

Kindness is listed as one of the nine "fruits of the Spirit," one of the nine characteristics of those who "live by the Spirit" and are "guided by the Spirit" (Galatians 5:22-25). Kindness is the goal of those who pray "your will be done, on earth . . ."

Jesus was kind. He told the crowds who gathered around him, "Come to me, all you that are weary and are carrying heavy burdens, and I will give you rest. Take my yoke upon you, and learn from me; for I am gentle and humble in heart, and you will find rest for your souls" (Matthew 11:28-29). Over and over again, we are told that when Jesus saw the crowds with their questions, their suffering, their need, "he had compassion for them" (Matthew 9:36; 14:14; 15:32). On two occasions, in arguments with religious leaders who were angry with Jesus for not being fussy about the "rules," Jesus said, "I desire mercy, not sacrifice" (Matthew 9:13; 12:7). Jesus did not have a rules-based understanding of religion; he had a relationship-based understanding. What was good for people mattered and so he told his followers, "Blessed are the merciful" (Matthew 5:7).

It is a radical kindness that Jesus asks of us for he knew that kindness as the will of God is rooted in the very nature of God: "But love your enemies, do good, and lend, expecting nothing in return. Your reward will be great, and you will be children of the Most High; for he is kind to the ungrateful and the wicked. Be merciful, just as your Father is merciful" (Luke 6:35-36). When we pray this prayer, we pray that we would come to see kindness not as law but as gospel, as a grace-inspired quality in human relationships that we seek to learn and to live.

Biblical Wisdom

Thus says the LORD of hosts: Render true judgments, show kindness and mercy to one another; do not oppress the widow, the orphan, the alien, or the poor; and do not devise evil in your hearts against one another.
  Zechariah 7:9-10 *But they refused to listen*

Theological Thoughts

When we pray "your will be done," we are not asking that things come out right as we want things to come out, but rather we are asking that God's will be done. Too often we are conditioned to think of prayer as asking God for what we want . . . But now, in praying that God's will be done on earth as it is in heaven, we are attempting to school ourselves to want what God wants.[24]

Silence for Meditation

Questions to Ponder

- Does it seem strange to you that kindness is included in the will of God? Why or why not?

- In our impersonal, high-stress, competitive world, kindness might seem a luxury we can ill afford. Is it? Why or why not?
- Jesus' words, "Be merciful just as your Father is merciful," seem difficult if not impossible to follow—and so we usually experience them as law. How might we come to experience them as grace?

Psalm Fragment
Teach me to do your will,
for you are my God.
Let your good spirit lead me
on a level path.
Psalm 143:10

Journal Reflections
- Write about a time when you were treated with unexpected kindness.
- Write about a time when you treated someone else with unexpected kindness.
- Do you find it as easy to be kind to strangers as to family and friends? Explain.

Prayer for Today
Jesus, let me bask in your kindness today and find rest for my soul. Amen.

Journey
Day 16—Saturday

Your will be done, on earth as in heaven.

If there is one thing that is clear from the beginning to the end of the Bible, it is that God desires to be in relationship with us. We have already seen that one of the things God wants from us is that we "walk humbly with [our] God." Throughout the Bible, God beseeches his people to "return" to God, return to following God. Isaiah 44:22 represents a constantly recurring refrain:

I have swept away your transgressions like a cloud,
>   and your sins like mist;
>   return to me, for I have redeemed you.

"Return to me, for I have redeemed you." When we pray that God's will be done on earth, we are praying that we (and everyone else) would return to God, trusting and celebrating the forgiveness and redemption that have been freely given to us.

Jesus came to make God known. He knew that the only truly human life is life lived with God, the only life that finally makes sense is life lived with God, the only life that truly is *life* is life lived with God.

On the night before he died, Jesus prayed for his disciples, "And this is eternal life, that they may know you, the only true God, and Jesus Christ whom you have sent" (John 17:3). Knowing God and following the God you know is what the life of faith is all about. Walking humbly with God—a life of prayer, immersion in the Bible, learning to love (1 John 4:7-8), and living faithfully—is the path to such knowledge. Walking that path is the will of God for us.

We might also say that God's will is that we should live lives that are good for us and good for others. Walking humbly with God is just such a life. As God said through the prophet Jeremiah, "For surely I know the plans I have for you, says the LORD, plans for your welfare and not for harm, to give you a future with hope" (29:11). When we pray that God's will be done on earth we pray for such a "future with hope," a future grounded in and dependent upon our deepening relationship with God.

> *Biblical Wisdom*
> *If we live by the Spirit, let us also be guided by the Spirit.*
> Galatians 5:25

> *Theological Thoughts*

To be human means to accept responsibility under God's mandate and according to his will (Gen. 1:26-28); and we are praying here simply that [we] will become human.[25]

Silence for Meditation

Questions to Ponder

- In what ways does your community of faith foster a humble walk with God?
- The text from Isaiah 44 declares that a return to God is possible because God has redeemed us. Redemption is grace. Why, therefore, is this text often heard as law?
- How do worship and the community activities of the church cultivate and nourish a humble walk with God?

Psalm Fragment
I delight to do your will, O my God;
your law is within my heart.
Psalm 40:8

Journal Reflections

- Write about times (and places) when you feel closest to God.
- Compare your present view of eternal life with Jesus' statement that eternal life is to know God and Jesus. What do you think "knowing" God means?
- Read 1 John 4:7-8 and write a short meditation about knowing God.

Worship Hints for Tomorrow

- Look at the people around you in worship. Pick one or two whose lives represent for you a breaking in of the kingdom. Tell them you feel that way.
- While waiting for church to begin, read the Sunday bulletin and church newsletter looking for examples of the ways in which the church does justice. Where might you get involved?

Prayer for Today

God, I do not know where today will take me. I only pray that, wherever I go, I walk with you. Amen.

Journey
Day 17—Monday

Your will be done, on earth as in heaven.

If God's will is that we should all walk humbly with our God, then God's will must be that those of us who are doing just that help others get to the same place. Not by coercion, not by buttonholing them, not by pestering or intimidating them—but by the persuasive power of love. As Jesus told his followers, "By this everyone will know that you are my disciples, if you have love for one another" (John 13:35).

According to Paul, God "reconciled us to himself through Christ, and has given us the ministry of reconciliation; that is, in Christ God was reconciling the world to himself, not counting their trespasses against them, and entrusting the message of reconciliation to us" (2 Corinthians 5:18-19). God's reconciling of the world was a pure act of love, and the message of that love is ours to live out and share in a largely loveless world. As Mother Teresa once said, we are all "a little pencil in the hands of a writing God who is sending a love letter to the world."[26]

Evangelism is at the heart of God's will for us. The word *evangelism*, however, troubles many Christians. It conjures up images of aggressive proselytizers, religious fanatics, or extremists who self-righteously demand to know if others are "saved." But this is not evangelism, and there is no need for people of faith to tremble at the sound of the word.

True evangelism is simply sharing in one way or another what's real for you. Evangelism is *speaking and living* the good news of God's love, God's justice, God's forgiveness, God's compassion, and God's salvation. Usually living the good news will come before speaking the good news. To paraphrase the saying "Build it and they will come," "Live it and they will ask about it." And then, with "gentleness and reverence," you simply give an account "for the hope that is in you," for the love that drives you, for the faith that gets you up in the morning and sees you through the day (1 Peter 3:15-16a). To pray that God's will be done on earth is to pray for the faith and courage both to live under the rule of God and to invite others to do the same.

Biblical Wisdom

But you are a chosen race, a royal priesthood, a holy nation, God's own people, in order that you may proclaim the mighty acts of him who called you out of darkness into his marvelous light.

1 Peter 2:9

Theological Thoughts

Prayer in Jesus' name is lifelong training in taking God's will a little more seriously and our own will a little less so.[27]

Silence for Meditation

Questions to Ponder

- How is God's will that Christians be evangelists expressed in your faith community?
- What do you think is the content of the "message of reconciliation" God has entrusted to us?
- Many Americans feel that faith is a private matter not to be shared. Do you agree? Why or why not?

Psalm Fragment

O give thanks to the LORD, call on his name,
    make known his deeds among the peoples.
Sing to him, sing praises to him;
    tell of all his wonderful works.
Glory in his holy name;
    let the hearts of those who seek the LORD rejoice.

Psalm 105:1-3

Journal Reflections

- Write about times when someone talked to you about things of faith. Were you open or closed, offended or interested? Why?
- In what ways are you a "pencil in the hands of a writing God who is sending a love letter to the world"?

- Write a short meditation on the hymn title "They Will Know We Are Christians by Our Love." What other ways might someone know we are Christian?

Prayer for Today

God of invitation, I want to live in such a way today that I am an expression of your message of reconciliation. Amen.

Journey

Day 18—Tuesday

Your will be done, on earth as in heaven.

Once when Jesus was asked if he was hungry, he said, "My food is to do the will of him who sent me" (John 4:34). He hungered and thirsted for God's will. We, on the other hand, hunger and thirst for so many things that have little if anything to do with God's will.

With our mouths we say the words "*your* will be done," but all too often our lives say "*my* will be done." If we are going to pray this prayer rightly, we will need to take Paul's advice seriously:

> Let each of you look not to your own interests, but to the interests of others. Let the same mind be in you that was in Christ Jesus, who, though he was in the form of God, did not regard equality with God as something to be exploited, but emptied himself, taking the form of a slave. (Philippians 2:4-7)

Impossible? It would seem so in our culture, which encourages us to be full of ourselves, self-centered, self-absorbed, selfish—quite the opposite of the mind of Jesus.

Paul's advice that we think with the mind of Christ, that we look first to the interests and needs of others, would indeed seem like hard, if not impossible, advice to follow if, six verses later, he had not written, "It is God who is at work in you, enabling you both to will and to work for his good pleasure" (Philippians 2:13). This is something that every baptized Christian should know, *claim*, and experience for themselves. God is at work in us.

Perfection is not in the cards for finite human beings. That being said, it is nevertheless true that, open to the enlivening, empowering, guiding presence of the Spirit of Christ within us, we are capable of living a lot closer to the will of God than we usually do.

Biblical Wisdom

As God's chosen ones, holy and beloved, clothe yourselves with compassion, kindness, humility, meekness, and patience.
Colossians 3:12

Theological Thoughts

Human resistance against God's will prevents it from being done. Human resistance is easily explained: it has its cause in human self-will. Thereby human self-will is pitted against God's will, and this rebellion is identical with sinfulness.[28]

see Jeek 7: 12ff -

Silence for Meditation

Questions to Ponder

- What are some of the major "hungers" and "thirsts" of our culture?
- What are the cultural values and forces that work against our having the "mind of Christ"?
- What would you say is evidence that God is at work in your faith community?

Psalm Fragment

I know that the LORD maintains the cause of the needy,
and executes justice for the poor.
Surely the righteous shall give thanks to your name;
the upright shall live in your presence.
Psalm 140:12-13

Journal Reflections

- As humans we hunger and thirst for many things—some of them not so good, some of them very good. Make a list of the good things you hunger and thirst for.
- Write a short meditation on having the mind of Christ.
- Make a list of the ways in which God is at work in you.

Prayer for Today

Holy God, help me to sort out my hungers and thirsts so I know which are in keeping with your will and which are not. Amen.

Journey Week Four

Days 19–24

Give us today our daily bread.

Journey
Day 19—Wednesday

Give us today our daily bread.

For the past three weeks we have focused on God's name, God's kingdom, and God's will. Now our focus shifts. In the last four petitions of the Lord's Prayer, our attention is drawn to human needs—our need for bread, our need for forgiveness, our need for rescue and deliverance.

First, we pray for "our daily bread." Again, the little word *our* is worth thinking about. Christian faith is personal in the sense that we all stand personally before God, are all loved personally by God, and are all personally called to follow Jesus in the way of God. But Christian faith is not individualistic. It is never only about me. We always stand before God as part of both the community of faith and the larger community of humankind. Christian faith connects us to everyone. When anyone suffers, we all suffer; when things go well for anyone, things go well for everyone. As the seventeenth-century English poet John Donne so beautifully put it:

> Any man's death diminishes me
> because I am involved in mankind.[29]

To be Christian is to be involved in humankind. In the Lord's Prayer, we do not pray for "my" bread; we pray for "our" bread. We pray that no one would go to bed hungry, would suffer from malnutrition, would die for lack of "bread."

The celebration of Holy Communion gives us a powerful symbol of what it means to pray for "our" bread. Have you noticed how the sacrament levels the playing field? The wealthy and the poor, the strong and the weak, the powerful and the powerless, those who have the "good life" and those for whom life is a constant struggle—everyone comes to the table of Christ and everyone eats. Everyone, regardless of his or her station in life, gets the same small piece of bread, the same small cup of wine. The "haves" do not get the whole loaf while the "have-nots" get the crumbs, as so often happens in the world outside the church. The bread and wine of Christ's presence is food for the journey, and no one gets left out.

When we pray for "our daily bread," we are praying that the fairness and justice of Holy Communion would become the fairness and justice of our world.

Biblical Wisdom

Those who are generous are blessed,
> *for they share their bread with the poor.*
Proverbs 22:9

Theological Thoughts

If hunger occurs the reason is most often that those who are expected to "give" refuse to give. The giving therefore depends not only on the production of the bread but also on the willingness to share it. Given the experience of human stinginess, one has every reason not to take human generosity for granted. God is therefore also asked to see to it that human providers are disposed in their hearts and minds to share what has been produced.[30]

Silence for Meditation

Questions to Ponder

- Do you agree that Christian faith is "personal" but not "individualistic"? Why?
- What does it mean to you to stand before God in the larger community of humankind?
- In what sense is John Donne correct when he says that anyone's death diminishes us?

Psalm Fragment

You cause the grass to grow for the cattle,
> *and plants for people to use,*
to bring forth food from the earth,
> *and wine to gladden the human heart,*
oil to make the face shine,
> *and bread to strengthen the human heart.*
Psalm 104:14-15

Journal Reflections

- In what ways have you experienced Christian faith as being deeply personal?
- Make a list of the ways you are involved in humankind.
- Does Holy Communion work for you as a symbol of justice and fairness? Why or why not?

Prayer for Today

Lord of the harvest, thank you for "bread to strengthen the human heart." May everyone's heart be strengthened with bread. Amen.

Journey
Day 20—Thursday

Give us today our daily bread.

Bread means bread—but it also means much more than bread. It is a metaphor for the material necessities of life. When we pray for daily bread, we recognize our dependence upon God for "bread," for all those things that sustain life, that bring security, that make the experience of being alive a good experience. For all too many people, the experience of being alive is not a good experience. And that matters to God.

Christianity cannot be reduced to a concern with spiritual things alone. It also has to do with the earthy, the fleshly, the bodily, the physical. When Jesus said, "I came that they may have life, and have it abundantly" (John 10:10), he wasn't only talking about eternal life, he was also talking about this bodily life we live right here and now.

This life we live right here and now is a gift of God, but it is a fragile, vulnerable gift—we so easily suffer and die from want of bread—and so we pray for daily bread, for whatever is needed to protect the gift. In the Hebrew book of Sirach (written about 180 B.C.E.) we are told, "The necessities of life are water, bread, and clothing, and also a house" (Sirach 29:21). In our globalizing world, we might add to the list: health care, education, the arts, equal opportunity, freedom from political and military violence; in short, whatever gives security, happiness, and meaning to human life. When we pray for daily bread, we pray for it all—for ourselves and for everyone else. No exceptions.

And it could be done. It is not a question of scarcity. God created our beautiful blue-green planet in such a way that it naturally provides in abundance all that is needed for all people to live well. God continues to give daily bread in abundance. The problem is one of distribution, and the will to distribute fairly. And that's our problem, not God's. And to overcome that problem, we pray for *our* daily bread.

Biblical Wisdom

And God is able to provide you with every blessing in abundance, so that by always having enough of everything, you may share abundantly in every good work. As it is written, "He scatters abroad, he gives to the poor; his righteousness endures forever."
   2 Corinthians 9:8-9

Theological Thoughts

[Daily bread means] everything included in the necessities and nourishment of our bodies, such as food, drink, clothing, shoes, house, farm, fields, livestock, money, property, an upright spouse, upright children, upright members of the household, upright and faithful rulers, good government, good weather, peace, health, decency, honor, good friends, faithful neighbors, and the like.[31]

Silence for Meditation

Questions to Ponder

· Look again at Luther's definition of daily bread in today's Theological Thoughts. Have you thought about "daily bread" this way before? Explain.
· What might you add to Luther's list to make it more twenty-first century?
· When it comes to people suffering for want of "bread," do you agree that it is a problem of distribution and not scarcity? Explain. Any suggestions for facing the distribution problem?

Psalm Fragment
These all look to you
> *to give them their food in due season;*
> *when you give to them, they gather it up;*
> *when you open your hand, they are filled with good things.*

Psalm 104:27-28

Journal Reflections

- Given Luther's definition of daily bread, how is your prayer for bread being answered?
- Write about your sense of the fragility and vulnerability of life.
- In what ways is your Christian faith concerned with the fleshly, the bodily, the physical?

Prayer for Today

Giving God, grant me and all people sufficient bread for the journey through life. Amen.

Journey
Day 21—Friday

Give us today our daily bread.

Could there be anything more important than food in making life worth living? Perhaps only one thing—food eaten together. From the family meal to the village festival, from dinner out with someone special to a lunch break in the cafeteria, from the church potluck to the wedding feast, from sitting around a campfire roasting hot dogs to inviting friends over for pizza—eating together is one of the best things we do.

Relationships are formed around food. We get to know each other, we discover our commonalities, we laugh and cry, we celebrate our joys and share our sorrows—all around food. In so many ways, sharing food is the "tie that binds" us together.

Jesus ate with anybody who would eat with him. And he was criticized for it. About himself he said, "The Son of Man came eating and drinking, and they say, 'Look, a glutton and a drunkard, a friend of tax collectors and sinners!'" (Matthew 11:19). No one was excluded from Jesus' table except those who excluded themselves. The only ones who didn't experience the good food, good wine, and good times at Jesus' table were those who thought they were too good to eat and drink (let alone talk to) the folks who joyfully sat down to the table with him.

Jesus' meals with "tax collectors and sinners" were a powerful symbol that in Jesus God's rule had begun. For centuries, the "great day of the Lord," the coming of God's kingdom had been symbolized by a great banquet where *everyone* had their fill of the finest food. One of the great prophecies of this "great day of the Lord" comes from the prophet Isaiah, and there is no doubt but that Jesus knew it well:

> On this mountain the LORD of hosts will make for all peoples
> a feast of rich food, a feast of well-aged wines,
> of rich food filled with marrow, of well-aged wines strained clear
> (Isaiah 25:6)

Jesus' open meals with "tax collectors and sinners" were a foretaste of this feast to come. *Our* daily bread, our meals together, are also a foretaste of the feast to come.

Biblical Wisdom

Now all the tax collectors and sinners were coming near to listen to him. And the Pharisees and the scribes were grumbling and saying, "This fellow welcomes sinners and eats with them."
   Luke 15:1-2

Theological Thoughts

Eating bread may be a physical act, but sharing bread is a spiritual act. Jesus hungers and thirsts for the new world of righteousness, and he acts ahead of time in the power of the coming world, eating with tax collectors and sinners, multiplying loaves for the hungry.[32]

Silence for Meditation

Questions to Ponder

- What do church potluck suppers have to do with Jesus' open meals?
- Do you like the idea that Jesus was criticized as a "glutton and a drunkard"? Explain.
- Why do you think that a banquet or feast was used as a symbol for the fulfillment of God's hope for the world?

Psalm Fragment

How precious is your steadfast love, O God!
   All people may take refuge in the shadow of your wings.
They feast on the abundance of your house,
   and you give them drink from the river of your delights.
For with you is the fountain of life;
   in your light we see light.
Psalm 36:7-9

Journal Reflections

- Write about your experience of church picnics and potluck suppers. Do they work for you as a symbol that in Jesus God's rule has begun? Why or why not?
- If you have ever served and/or eaten at a homeless shelter, write about the experience. What feelings did it evoke? If you haven't, why not give it a try?
- Whom we will eat with and whom we won't eat with can tell us a lot about ourselves. Make a list of specific people you will and won't eat with. Any conclusions?

Prayer for Today

God of such abundance, thank you for common meals in which that abundance is shared. Amen.

Journey
Day 22—Saturday

Give us today our daily bread.

It is possible to make too much of bread—both in its literal and figurative sense. It is also possible to confuse needs with wants.

We have noted that "bread" is a metaphor for the material necessities of life. Safe and nutritious food is a necessity. A $200 meal is not. Safe and clean water is a necessity. "Designer" water is not. A good and safe place to live is a necessity. A million dollar house is not. A safe way to get where we need to go is a necessity. A $75,000 automobile is not. Safe and affordable health care is a necessity. Elective cosmetic surgery is not. When we make too much of "bread" and confuse genuine needs with wants, we make a mess of things for ourselves and others. We get distracted by things that might be nice to have but really don't matter, and in our distraction we miss much of what makes life truly meaningful and happy.

At the beginning of his ministry, Jesus went into the wilderness to pray and to confront the temptations that are common to human kind. He ate nothing during his time in the wilderness, and when it was almost over he was famished. "The tempter came and said to him, 'If you are the Son of God, command these stones to become loaves of bread.' But he answered, 'It is written, 'One does not live by bread alone, but by every word that comes from the mouth of God'" (Matthew 4:3-4).

We are strange creatures. On the one hand, we are flesh and blood, biological creatures who cannot live without "bread." On the other hand, "bread alone" is not enough. We are *ensouled* flesh and blood, spiritual creatures who truly cannot live without "every word that comes from the mouth of God"—words such as "love, joy, peace, patience, kindness, generosity, faithfulness, gentleness, and self-control" (the fruit of the Spirit in Galatians 5:22-23).

When we pray for our daily bread, we should not make too much of bread; we should remember that "bread alone" is not enough, and so we should also pray for the "fruit of the Spirit."

Biblical Wisdom
No, the word is very near to you; it is in your mouth and in your heart for
you to observe.
 Deuteronomy 30:14

Theological Thoughts

We come to prayer aware of urgent needs, or at least wants. It is tempting to race through the Lord's Prayer, as far as "on earth as it is in heaven," so that we can then take a deep breath and say, "Now look here: when it comes to daily bread, there are some things I simply must have." And then off we go into a shopping list. To do this, of course, is to let greed get in the way of grace.[33]

Silence for Meditation

Questions to Ponder

· In what ways does our culture "make too much of bread"?
· What criteria can we use to distinguish between real needs and wants?
· How do we "consume" every word that comes out of the mouth of God?

Psalm Fragment
Your word is a lamp to my feet
 and a light to my path.
 Psalm 119:105

Journal Reflections

· Make a list of strategies you might employ to help you not make too much of bread.
· Write about the role of the Bible in your life of faith.
· Are you satisfied with the amount of time you spend reading the Bible? Explain.

Worship Hints for Tomorrow

· Listen for words and look for symbols of invitation and welcome during worship and in the church.

- As you go to and return from Christ's table, look at the people around you. Whom could you invite to a meal that you've never eaten with before (except at Christ's table)?

Prayer for Today

God, nourish me with your Word, sustain me with your Word, correct me with your Word, guide me with your Word. Amen.

Journey
Day 23—Monday

Give us today our daily bread.

Today we ponder a much deeper meaning to the prayer for daily bread. Yesterday we noted that we do not live by bread alone, "but by every word that comes from the mouth of God" (Matthew 4:4). This can be taken to mean that we live by Jesus, the "Word [that] became flesh and lived among us" (John 1:14). Jesus is Word of God—the one who makes God known.

In the mystical and poetically beautiful language of St. John's Gospel, Jesus declares, "I am the bread of life. Whoever comes to me will never be hungry, and whoever believes in me will never be thirsty" (John 6:35).

We hunger and thirst for so much and so much of what we hunger and thirst for does not satisfy. So much of our time, so much of our work, so much of our efforts and planning go into securing this, that, or the next thing that we hope will satisfy our hunger—but they don't.

Our true hunger is for God, and the baubles of our culture will not satisfy this hunger. As St. Augustine wrote in the fourth century, "God, you have made us for yourself, and our hearts are restless till they find their rest in you."[34] Our prayer for daily bread must be accompanied by the recognition that bread alone will not fill the gnawing emptiness within.

The prophet Isaiah well understood this human restlessness that only God can still:

Ho, everyone who thirsts,
> come to the waters;
> and you that have no money,
> come, buy and eat!
Come, buy wine and milk
> without money and without price.
Why do you spend your money for that which is not bread,
> and your labor for that which does not satisfy? (Isaiah 55:1-2)

He asks a good question—one that we who labor mightily might well ponder. The road to that which finally satisfies our hunger, which finally stills our restlessness, which finally makes sense out of our lives runs through Jesus. When we pray for daily bread, we are also praying for the "bread of life," for a deepening, nourishing, enlivening relationship with Jesus, the self-disclosure of God.

Biblical Wisdom

Abide in me as I abide in you. Just as the branch cannot bear fruit by itself unless it abides in the vine, neither can you unless you abide in me. I am the vine, you are the branches. Those who abide in me and I in them bear much fruit, because apart from me you can do nothing.
> John 15:4-5

Theological Thoughts

And yet this may be a petition for spiritual bread, for the presence of Jesus himself, Wisdom incarnate, who issues the invitation to come and take his yoke, to enter his presence, to receive him as food and drink.[35]

Silence for Meditation

Questions to Ponder

- What does the image of vine and branches tell you about our relationship with Jesus?
- What cultural evidence is there of the "restlessness" of the human heart?
- How do we know when our hunger has been satisfied, our thirst quenched, our restless heart finally at rest?

Psalm Fragment
As a deer longs for flowing streams,
so my soul longs for you, O God.
My soul thirsts for God,
for the living God.
When shall I come and behold
the face of God?
Psalm 42:1-2

Journal Reflections

· Write about the ways in which today's *Psalm Fragment* speaks to you.
· What strategies do you have for abiding in Jesus?
· Write a prayer or psalm expressing your particular longing for God.

Prayer for Today

Jesus, teach me what it means to abide in you, to be nourished in you, to bear fruit in you. Amen.

Journey
Day 24—Tuesday

Give us today our daily bread.

When Jesus taught his followers to pray for daily bread, he probably did not have the sacrament of Holy Communion in mind. Given the nature of Jesus' own life and teaching, his command that we pray for daily bread was most likely a command that we pray for simple ordinary bread, food for the day, the material necessities of life.

Nevertheless, the experience of the church in the years following Jesus' death and resurrection has encouraged people of faith to see the daily bread for which we pray *both* as ordinary bread and as the bread of Christ's presence in Holy Communion. We pray for ordinary bread to strengthen our bodies. We pray for the bread of Christ's presence to sustain our spirits.

When we come to the table of Christ to receive bread and wine, our minds (and faith) are drawn in three directions—the past, the future, and the present. When Jesus blessed bread and wine and gave it to his followers during his last supper, he told them to eat and drink to remember him (Luke 22:19). When we come to the table of Christ, we come remembering what Jesus said and what he did, how he lived and how he died, and why.

After giving his followers the bread and wine, Jesus said to them, "I tell you, I will never again drink of this fruit of the vine until that day when I drink it new *with you* in my Father's kingdom" (Matthew 26:29) (italics added). When we come to the table of Christ, we come anticipating the great feast when "people will come from east and west, from north and south, and will eat in the kingdom of God" (Luke 13:29).

In speaking of the sacramental bread, Paul declares, "Because there is one bread, we who are many are one body, for we all partake of the one bread" (1 Corinthians 10:17). When we come to the table of Christ, we don't come alone. We come as "one body," men and women and children bound to each other in the present moment as those who need the spiritually nourishing "daily bread" of Christ's presence in order that together we might have the faith, strength, and courage to daily follow Jesus in the way of God.

When we come to the Lord's table for daily bread, we come remembering, anticipating, and following.

> *Biblical Wisdom*
> *They devoted themselves to the apostles' teaching and fellowship, to the breaking of bread and the prayers.*
> Acts 2:42

> *Theological Thoughts*

When we want to meet God, we Christians do not go up some high mountain, do not rummage around in our psyches, do not hold hands, close our eyes, and sing Kum Ba Yah in the hope of revelation. We gather and break bread in Jesus' name. That's where he has chosen to meet us, that's where our eyes are opened and we recognize him.[36]

Silence for Meditation

Questions to Ponder

- Does it make sense to you to add Holy Communion to the meaning of "daily bread"? Why?
- Usually we think of communion in terms of remembrance. Do you agree that communion also focuses our attention on the present and the future? Explain.
- What does it mean to say that because we all eat of the "one bread" we are all bound together in "one body"?

Psalm Fragment

Happy is everyone who fears the LORD,
*   who walks in his ways.*
You shall eat the fruit of the labor of your hands;
*   you shall be happy, and it shall go well with you.*
    Psalm 128:1-2

Journal Reflections

- Write a short meditation on the experience of Holy Communion for you.
- At communion, do you usually focus on remembering, anticipating, or following? Explain.
- What is the significance for you of the fact that you never go to the table of Christ alone?

Prayer for Today

Enlivening God, thank you for satisfying my hungry soul with bread of Christ's presence. Amen.

Journey Week Five

Days 25–30

Forgive us our sins as we forgive those who sin against us.

Journey
Day 25—Wednesday

Forgive us our sins as we forgive those who sin against us.

The fifth petition in our Lord's Prayer is about a subject dear to the heart of Jesus—forgiveness. Jesus both declared divine forgiveness (for example, Luke 7:47; Matthew 9:2) and called his followers to be people who forgive (for example, Mark 11:25; Matthew 18:21-22). He saw forgiveness as a two-way street: God freely forgives us, and, within the ethos of divine forgiveness, we freely forgive others. That's just how things are under the rule of God.

Although Matthew's Greek is often translated "Forgive us our trespasses," the word literally means "debts." In this prayer we ask God to forgive our debts as we forgive those who are indebted to us. In Luke's version of the Lord's Prayer, we ask God to "forgive our sins, for we ourselves forgive everyone *indebted* to us." So what is all this talk about debts?

It doesn't take a great stretch of the imagination to realize that we are deeply indebted to God. God has created this planet in such a way that it bountifully provides all that is needed for a meaningful and happy life for all people. We are in debt to God in that we have a moral obligation to recognize God's beneficence with the gratitude it deserves. We rarely do. We "owe" God trust and love and a life lived in keeping with God's gracious will—it is a debt that keeps growing as we turn our trust and love toward the things of this world rather than toward the creator of this world.

God deals equitably with us and expects us to deal equitably with each other—our lack of justice is rolled into the debt that we owe God. God has compassion on us and treats us with mercy—our indifference to others adds to the debt that we owe to God.

Our failure to pay our moral obligations, our "debt" to God, is one way to define sin, and that is why in some translations of the Lord's Prayer we ask God to forgive our "sin," and in others we ask God to forgive us our "trespasses" (a word that literally means "to commit an offense, to transgress, to sin").

Our debt to God is so great that we cannot repay it, and so we have no recourse but to ask for forgiveness—a forgiveness that God is quick to grant (for example, Luke 23:34; 2 Corinthians 5:18-19; Psalm 103:10-12). In granting forgive-ness, God grants the gift of relationship, the gift of a future not chained to or determined by the debts and sins of the past.

Biblical Wisdom
If we say that we have no sin, we deceive ourselves, and the truth is not in us. If we confess our sins, he who is faithful and just will forgive us our sins and cleanse us from all unrighteousness.
  1 John 1:8-9

Theological Thoughts
We ask in this prayer that our heavenly Father would not regard our sins nor deny these petitions on their account, for we are worthy of nothing for which we ask, nor have we earned it. Instead we ask that God would give us all things by grace, for we daily sin much and deserve only punishment. So, on the other hand, we, too, truly want to forgive heartily and to do good gladly to those who sin against us.[37]

Silence for Meditation

Questions to Ponder
· Which word do you prefer: trespasses, sins, or debts? Why?
· In Matthew's Gospel, why do you think Jesus used a word that literally means "debt" instead of a word that literally means "sin"?
· Does it make you feel any different asking God to forgive your debts instead of sin? Explain.

Psalm Fragment
  O you who answer prayer!
To you all flesh shall come.
When deeds of iniquity overwhelm us,
    you forgive our transgressions.
  Psalm 65:2-3

Journal Reflections

- Is this petition a word of grace or a word of law to you? Explain.
- Make a list of the debts you owe to God. In a prayer of confession, read the list to God.
- Draw a line through each debt and write canceled over the list. You are free of debt.

Prayer for Today

Forgiving God, thank you for removing the weight of my debt. Amen.

Journey
Day 26—Thursday

Forgive us our sins as we forgive those who sin against us.

If we are in debt to God and in need of God's forgiveness, then it stands to reason that we are in debt to each other and in need of each other's forgiveness. Our failure to love each other as God loves us runs up our debt to God while at the same time running up our debt to each other.

As St. Paul wrote, "Owe no one anything, *except* to love one another" (Romans 13:8) (italics added). When we do not love, we are in debt to those we owe love. When we are not loved, those who have failed to love us are in debt to us. We cannot pay the accumulated debt, and neither can they. The only answer to this spiral of debt is forgiveness, a clean slate, a fresh start, a renewed relationship.

As God forgives our sins, we forgive those who sin against us, and we pray that those we have sinned against will do the same—forgive us. As this cycle of forgiveness replaces the spiral of debt, everything old passes away, everything becomes new (2 Corinthians 5:16-19).

Lots of ink has been spilled trying to explain away the apparent conditional nature of God's forgiveness in this petition. It can be (and has been) argued that God will forgive us only to the degree that we forgive others. That would suggest, however, that our forgiveness of others *earns* God's forgiveness of us. Such an interpretation smacks of "works righteousness," the notion that human behavior trumps God's grace and "merits" God's forgiveness, salvation, blessing. It doesn't.

We forgive as a grateful response to God's already granted forgiveness, and in recognition of the fact that forgiveness is the royal road to renewed relationships. That God freely forgives us in no way means that sin doesn't matter to God. It does, and so do sin's consequences, which usually continue way past forgiveness—consequences that demand our attention.

God forgives, not in spite of sin, but because of sin. Sin is a disrupter and destroyer of relationships and God wants a healthy relationship with us. And so God forgives. God wants us to have healthy relationships with each other. And so God calls us to forgive as we have been forgiven. When we pray this petition, we are saying, "God, you keep on forgiving us and we'll keep on forgiving others because that's the only thing that makes sense in a broken world."

Biblical Wisdom
But God proves his love for us in that while we still were sinners Christ died for us.
Romans 5:8

Theological Thoughts
In the cancellation of debt that cannot possibly be paid back, God provides the indebted with a new start, a new start characterized by the transformation of the radically forgiven into those who also radically forgive.[38]

Silence for Meditation

Questions to Ponder
- In what ways are our debt to God and our debt to each other interrelated?
- How does forgiveness break the spiral of debt?
- What does it mean to say that God forgives *because* of sin and not *in spite* of sin?

Psalm Fragment

If you, O LORD, should mark iniquities,
Lord, who could stand?
But there is forgiveness with you.
Psalm 130:3-4a

Journal Reflections

- Do you usually experience yourself as a forgiving person or an unforgiving person? Explain.
- Write about a time when you needed and were graciously given forgiveness.
- Recall a time when you forgave someone. What was the impact on your relationship?

Prayer for Today

Forgiving God, as far as it depends upon me, may there be forgiveness in all my relationships. Amen.

Journey
Day 27—Friday

Forgive us our sins as we forgive those who sin against us.

Relationships matter to God—and so relationships should matter to us. "Beloved, since God loved us so much, we also ought to love one another" (1 John 4:11). It is important to remember this. Much damage has been done by those who think God cares more about "the rules" than relationships.

Once Jesus told his followers, "So when you are offering your gift at the altar, if you remember that your brother or sister has something against you, leave your gift there before the altar and go; first be reconciled to your brother or sister, and then come and offer your gift" (Matthew 5:23-24).

Imagine a pastor confronting a man who shows up in church on a Sunday morning, offering in hand, scowl on his face, and his wife absent. The pastor asks where his wife is; he responds that they had an argument and are not talking to each other. Now imagine the pastor telling him, "Well, take your offering with you and get out of here! Go back to your wife, make it right with her, and then come together, hand in hand, with your offering." Hard to imagine, isn't it? And yet that is exactly what Jesus told his followers to do.

Jesus once told Peter that if someone kept sinning against him, he should just keep forgiving (Matthew 18:21-22). Relationships are that important.

Such gratuitous forgiveness neither condones the offense that is forgiven nor welcomes continued offense. Forgiveness takes the offense with great seriousness, but takes the relationships involved with equally great seriousness. Forgiveness does not necessarily restore a broken relationship (some relationships are so destructive they are better not restored), but it does create the conditions for people to make new, better, more just choices and, thus, to make new relationships.

Jesus counseled against the ancient but conventional wisdom of "an eye for an eye and a tooth for a tooth"—or as we say today, "Don't get mad, get even." He substituted for it the unconventional wisdom that calls us to love our enemies and do good to those who would harm us (Matthew 5:38-45; cf. Romans 12:17-21). As Mahatma Gandhi reportedly said, "An eye for an eye makes the whole world blind."

Biblical Wisdom

Put away from you all bitterness and wrath and anger and wrangling and slander, together with all malice, and be kind to one another, tenderhearted, forgiving one another, as God in Christ has forgiven you.
Ephesians 4:31-32

Theological Thoughts

In commanding us to forgive, Jesus is inviting us to take charge, to turn the world around, to throw a monkey wrench in the eternal wheel of retribution and vengeance.[39]

Silence for Meditation

- In what ways does our culture discourage rather than encourage forgiveness?
- Are there some sins (and thus people) that should not be forgiven? Explain.
- Are relationships really as important as Jesus makes them out to be? Why or why not?

Psalm Fragment

Happy are those whose transgression is forgiven,
> *whose sin is covered.*
Psalm 32:1

Journal Reflections

- Write a short meditation exploring your understanding of today's *Biblical Wisdom*.
- What do you think of Jesus' unconventional wisdom that calls us to love our enemies?
- Have you ever followed the maxim "Don't get mad, get even!"? If so, what happened?

Prayer for Today

Jesus, grant me the courage to say "I'm sorry" and the courage to say "I forgive you" whenever these words need to be said. Amen.

Journey
Day 28—Saturday

Forgive us our sins as we forgive those who sin against us.

Forgiveness is dynamic, always happening, always needing to happen because we live in a far-less-than perfect world and we are far-less-than perfect people. Like daily bread, which we share with others as an expression of God's justice, we receive forgiveness daily, and we share it with others as an expression of God's love. How could we not? We have been given a chance to get things right. How could we deny that chance to others?

In the Gospel of John, we are told of a woman, caught in the act of adultery, who was dragged by a group of angry men to Jesus. They reminded Jesus that the law commanded them to stone such a woman to death. They stood there, stones in hand, wanting to know if he agreed.

In the anger-filled silence that followed their question, "Jesus bent down and wrote with his finger on the ground." The text doesn't tell us what he wrote, but I wouldn't be surprised if he scratched "Where's the man?" into the dust. Be that as it may, Jesus finally stood up and said to them, "Let anyone among you who is without sin be the first to throw a stone at her." He bent down again and went back to writing in the dirt. Again we don't know what he wrote, but I wonder if it might have had something to do with God's mercy, compassion, forgiveness.

One by one, the men dropped their stones and left. Jesus looked up and said to the woman: "Has no one condemned you?" She said, "No one, sir." To which Jesus replied, "Neither do I condemn you. Go your way, and from now on do not sin again" (John 8:2-11). She was not condemned; we are not condemned; we are not to condemn. She was given the freedom to make new and better choices; we are given the same freedom and expected to offer that freedom to others.

Biblical Wisdom
My friends, if anyone is detected in a transgression, you who have received the Spirit should restore such a one in a spirit of gentleness.
Galatians 6:1

Theological Thoughts
Forgiveness undermines the foundations of the old world and brings into being a new community. But the new community still inhabits the old world and the old world still inhabits the new people. Forgiveness, like bread, must be received day by day. And like bread, it is given to be shared. Sharing can never diminish love or forgiveness.[40]

Silence for Meditation

Questions to Ponder

- What do you make of the fact that the woman caught red-handed in the act of adultery was not condemned by Jesus?
- Luther said that the law should be used to restrain the wicked (civil use of the law). Does this contradict Jesus' teaching? Why or why not?
- How can someone be both forgiven and held responsible for their actions?

Psalm Fragment

Have mercy on me, O God,
  according to your steadfast love;
according to your abundant mercy
  blot out my transgressions.
Wash me thoroughly from my iniquity,
  and cleanse me from my sin.
For I know my transgressions,
  and my sin is ever before me.
  Psalm 51:1-3

Journal Reflections

- What feelings are evoked in you by the story of the woman caught in adultery?
- Was Jesus right not to condemn her? Why or why not?
- How does the story impact your view on the moral failures of others? On your own moral failures?

Worship Hints for Tomorrow

- If you are headed to church with a spouse, child, or friend whom you have something against (or who has something against you), stop the car, get reconciled, and then go to church.
- As you walk from the parking lot to the church, mentally drop any "stones" you are carrying.

Prayer for Today

Uncondemning God, if I am carrying any stones today, help me to drop them. Amen.

Journey
Day 29—Monday

Forgive us our sins as we forgive those who sin against us.

One of Jesus' most loved stories is the parable of the prodigal son. The younger son in this story deeply insulted his father by asking for his share of the inheritance while his father was still alive. It was a slap in the face, tantamount to saying, "I wish you were dead."

The father gave him what he wanted, and with it the freedom to choose a life quite different from what his father hoped for him. The word *prodigal* means wasteful, reckless, dissolute, profligate, uncontrolled, spendthrift, squanderer, self-indulgent, immoral, debauched. He was all of that. Totally self-absorbed. Not the kind of boy to make his father proud—and yet the father loved him.

His life goes from complete self-indulgence to self-pity when his money runs out and his "friends" run away. Close to starvation, he comes to his senses and realizes that his father's hired hands had plenty to eat while he has nothing. So he decides to go home, hat in hand. On the return journey he practices what he will say to his father: "Father, I have sinned against heaven and before you; I am no longer worthy to be called your son; treat me like one of your hired hands." The way the story is told, it is easy to see that he probably doesn't mean it. His confession is little more than a ruse to get him back in his father's good graces.

He needn't have worried. While he is still a ways off, his father sees him, is filled with compassion, runs to him, and kisses him before the boy can get a word of his confession out! He was forgiven, welcomed home, given the opportunity and responsibility to make new and better choices (Luke 15:11-32). And Jesus is telling us, *That's what God is like!*

And we need to be told. Human history demonstrates that we have a tendency to project our own smallness onto God. We think of God as angry and condemning, wrathful, bitter, resentful, needing to be appeased. But that's not the way God is and it's not the way we should be. As Jesus told those whose image of God was skewed, "Go and learn what this means, 'I desire mercy, not sacrifice'" (Matthew 9:13).

Biblical Wisdom
Blessed are the merciful, for they will receive mercy.
    Matthew 5:7

Theological Thoughts
Our relationship to God can be healthy only when our relationship to [others] is love; and both the earliest effort and latest fruit of love is forgiveness.[41]

Silence for Meditation

Questions to Ponder
- Was the father in the story of the prodigal son wrong to give the boy the money (and thus the freedom) so he could make his own lifestyle choices? Explain.
- What "inheritance" has God given us that we tend to misuse?
- In what ways must freedom and forgiveness go hand in hand?

Psalm Fragment
Then I acknowledged my sin to you,
        and I did not hide my iniquity;
I said, "I will confess my transgressions to the LORD,"
        and you forgave the guilt of my sin.
    Psalm 32:5

Journal Reflections
- Write a short meditation titled "The Upside and the Downside of Freedom."
- In what ways (if any) can you identify with the prodigal son?
- Imagine yourself in a similar situation to the father in the story. What would you do?

Prayer for Today
Jesus, thank you for giving me the space to learn from my own mistakes. Amen.

Journey
Day 30—Tuesday

Forgive us our sins as we forgive those who sin against us.

During the last moments of his life, Jesus was faced with a situation that would raise an unforgiving spirit in most of us—he was being murdered. The soldiers mocked him and beat him and nailed him to a cross. The crowds who watched were complicit in their silence. The religious leaders who had arranged for this most unfitting end to a good life hurled words of scorn and humiliation at him. And Jesus, looking out over it all, said, "Father, forgive them; for they do not know what they are doing" (Luke 23:34). And then a short time later, he cried out in a loud voice, "Father, into your hands I commend my spirit" (Luke 23:46), and he died.

"Father, forgive them; for they do not know what they are doing." Many years ago, on a Good Friday evening, sitting in the silence of a dimly lit sanctuary, listening to this text being read, it suddenly struck me that no one had asked for forgiveness! No one. No one in the crowds, none of the religious leaders, certainly not the soldiers. No one had asked for forgiveness and yet forgiveness had been given. Such is the way of God.

By speaking the word of forgiveness before anyone even acknowledged the need for forgiveness, Jesus created a sphere of forgiveness into which anyone could walk—and anyone who entered that sphere of forgiveness was free from the weight of sin, free to begin again. And it is worth noting that everyone who truly enters the sphere of forgiveness, everyone who truly breathes the air of God's mercy, forgives even as they have been forgiven.

As if to illustrate the power of unasked-for-forgiveness to create a sphere of forgiveness in which those who enter are free to begin again, Luke tells the story of the two thieves crucified with Jesus. One of the criminals mocked Jesus, but the other stepped into the sphere of forgiveness created when Jesus said, "Father, forgive them." He said, "Jesus, remember me when you come into your kingdom." And Jesus said, "Truly I tell you, today you will be with me in Paradise"

(Luke 23:42-43). One criminal died alone, filled with anger, hatred, fear. The other died in the embrace of a loving relationship. Both had received unasked-for-forgiveness; only one entered the sphere of forgiveness that Jesus opened up for both of them, and that made all the difference.

Biblical Wisdom

I will put my law within them, and I will write it on their hearts; and I will be their God, and they shall be my people. No longer shall they teach one another, or say to each other, "Know the LORD," for they shall all know me, from the least of them to the greatest, says the LORD; for I will forgive their iniquity, and remember their sin no more.

Jeremiah 31:33a-34

Theological Thoughts

Yet even at the point of his death Jesus declared his outpoured blood to be a strong tide able to destroy every barrier to the presence of God, washing clean the entire slate of debts, purging away accumulated pollution. In short, his blood was for the forgiveness of sins.[42]

Silence for Meditation

Questions to Ponder

- What happens when someone is told they are forgiven before they even ask for forgiveness?
- How can silence make someone complicit in evil?
- It could be said that the criminal who asked Jesus to remember him had a "deathbed conversion." Does that seem fair? Why or why not?

Psalm Fragment

Create in me a clean heart, O God,
    and put a new and right spirit within me.
Do not cast me away from your presence,
    and do not take your holy spirit from me.

Restore to me the joy of your salvation,
and sustain in me a willing spirit.
Psalm 51:10-12

Journal Reflections

- Do you experience Jesus' unasked-for-forgiveness as gospel or law—or both? Explain.
- Has anyone ever surprised you with a word of forgiveness you hadn't asked for and perhaps didn't even know you needed? If so, what was the experience like?
- Write a paragraph beginning with the words, "I forgive you, but . . . " Where did that line of thought take you? Anywhere close to where Jesus' way of forgiveness took him?

Prayer for Today

God of mercy, let there be no "buts" in my words of forgiveness. Amen.

Journey Week Six

Days 31–36

Save us from the time of trial...

Journey
Day 31—Wednesday

Save us from the time of trial . . .

The words of the sixth petition could be read as, "Lead us not into temptation," or "And do not bring us to the time of trial" or "Save us from the time of trial." Which leads to an important question: Does God *lead* us or *bring* us into temptation or trial? The Old Testament tradition thought so—sometimes directly (for example, Genesis 22:1-2; Exodus 16:4; Psalm 26:2), and sometimes indirectly, as in the book of Job where God allowed Satan to test Job severely. At first glance, Jesus' prayer seems to reflect this ancient tradition. But this tradition raises a problem.

Given that temptation is the temptation to sin, and given that we all too often give into temptations, if God leads us into them, wouldn't that make God complicit in evil? Given that the trial or test is to see whether or not we will follow the will and way of God, and given that we all too often fail the test, wouldn't that make God culpable in our fall into sin? It would seem so, but that's not something that people who believe in the righteousness of God want to say. And so we find James saying:

> No one, when tempted, should say, "I am being tempted by God"; for God cannot be tempted by evil and he himself tempts no one. But one is tempted by one's own desire, being lured and enticed by it; then, when that desire has conceived, it gives birth to sin, and that sin, when it is fully grown, gives birth to death. Do not be deceived, my beloved. (James 1:13-16)

Which is to say that God is responsible only in the sense that (for reasons known only to God) God allows evil to exist. God does not directly or indirectly tempt or test humankind, but in a world where God's name is not perfectly hallowed, where God's kingdom has not perfectly come, and God's will is not perfectly done, the threats and enticements of evil confront everyone, and every day we are tempted to yield. In this prayer we pray that God would both protect us as we face this inevitability and give us the wisdom and strength to make good choices, choices that mirror the will and way of God disclosed by Jesus.

Biblical Wisdom

So if you think you are standing, watch out that you do not fall. No testing has overtaken you that is not common to everyone. God is faithful, and he will not let you be tested beyond your strength, but with the testing he will also provide the way out so that you may be able to endure it.
1 Corinthians 10:12-13

Theological Thoughts

It is true that God tempts no one, but we ask in this prayer that God would preserve and keep us, so that the devil, the world, and our flesh may not deceive us or mislead us into false belief, despair, and other great shame and vice, and that, although we may be attacked by them, we may finally prevail and gain the victory.[43]

Silence for Meditation

Questions to Ponder

- Do you agree that God does not lead us or bring us into temptation or trial? Why or why not?
- Today's *Biblical Wisdom* states that God *allows* us to be tested, but won't let us be tested beyond our capacity to endure. What are the practical implications of that?
- In today's *Theological Thought*, what does Luther mean when he lists "despair" as a temptation that we ask God to protect us from?

Psalm Fragment
Prove me, O LORD, and try me;
test my heart and mind.
For your steadfast love is before my eyes,
and I walk in faithfulness to you.
Psalm 26:2-3

Journal Reflections

- Have you ever felt that God was testing you or allowing you to be tested? If so, describe the experience. What was the test? How did you handle it? What was the outcome?
- In times of temptation, testing, or trial, what spiritual resources do you rely on to help you?
- In the midst of a trial or temptation, have you ever talked about it with a pastor or trusted spiritual friend? If so, did it help? If not, why not give it a try?

Prayer for Today

God, don't let me make any choices today that would harm my relationship with you. Amen.

Journey
Day 32—Thursday

Save us from the time of trial . . .

Once again, we discover a plural pronoun. We do not pray "save *me* from the time of trial." We pray "save *us*" (which, of course, includes "me"). And again we are reminded that Christian faith is not solitary faith, it is not individualistic faith—it is always faith in community, faith with others, faith in solidarity with everyone who has ever been enticed or attacked by evil (and that's everyone!).

Jesus clearly understood the radically relational nature of human life. Nothing happens in a vacuum. What I do impacts others; what others do impacts me. What happens to me affects others; what happens to others affects me. As Paul noted, in the body of Christ (the church), "if one member suffers, all suffer together . . . ; if one member is honored, all rejoice together" (1 Corinthians 12:26). The same can be said of the larger body of humankind. And so we pray "save *us* from the time of trial," for whenever anyone is hurt by evil, we are all hurt.

Nobody is immune to the lure of temptation. No one is immune to the enticements and attacks of evil. We know from our own experience and the experience of others how easy it is to give in to temptation; we know from our own experience and the experience of others how quickly and tragically evil can strike. All of which suggests that, rather than disdain for the failings of others, and rather than indifference for the plight of others, empathy, compassion, and a strong feeling of solidarity with our fellow humans are in order.

And so we pray for each other, not wanting anyone to be tempted into the arms of evil or fall victim to those who have. When one suffers, we all suffer. When it goes well with one, it goes better for us all.

Biblical Wisdom

Pray in the Spirit at all times in every prayer and supplication. To that end keep alert and always persevere in supplication for all the saints.
Ephesians 6:18

Theological Thoughts

Jesus is calling his disciples to pray for deliverance from and protection in testing, not proposing that his disciples can avoid tests of their faith.[44]

Silence for Meditation

Questions to Ponder

- In what practical ways can a community of faith provide help in the face of temptation?
- Churches, like all institutions, are also subject to temptations, testing, and trials. What resources are available to help the church?
- Do you see any upside to the experience of temptation, testing, and trials? Explain.

Psalm Fragment

How very good and pleasant it is
when kindred live together in unity!
Psalm 133:1

Journal Reflections

- Write about an experience of being hurt when someone else gave in to temptation.
- Write about an experience when your giving into temptation hurt someone else.
- Write a prayer expressing your solidarity with others in the face of temptation and trials.

Prayer for Today

Gracious God, in times of trial and temptation, keep me focused on what keeps me close to you. Amen.

Journey
Day 33—Friday

Save us from the time of trial . . .

The Lord's Prayer is for ordinary people—not spiritual athletes.

Once Jesus told this story: "Two men went up to the temple to pray, one a Pharisee and the other a tax collector. The Pharisee, standing by himself, was praying thus, 'God, I thank you that I am not like other people: thieves, rogues, adulterers, or even like this tax collector. I fast twice a week; I give a tenth of all my income.' But the tax collector, standing far off, would not even look up to heaven, but was beating his breast and saying, 'God, be merciful to me, a sinner!'" (Luke 18:10-13). The Lord's Prayer is for folks like the tax collector.

It is for women and men who know they are able to make choices but also know that they often make the wrong choices in spite of their best intentions. It is for women and men who work hard to build a good and secure life but who also know that in many ways they are simply not in control.

About himself, St. Paul wrote:

I do not understand my own actions. For I do not do what I want, but I do the very thing I hate . . . I can will what is right, but I cannot do it. For I do not do the good I want, but the evil I do not want is what I do. Now if I do what I do not want, it is no longer I that do it, but sin that dwells within me. (Romans 7:15-20)

The Lord's Prayer was for Paul—and for folks who read his words and nod their heads in agreement.

It is for people who try and sometimes fail and feel bad about it. It is for people who have felt the pull of obsessive compulsive or addictive behaviors and can't resist them and feel bad about it. It is for people who know Jesus was talking to them when he said to his followers, "Stay awake and pray that you may not come into the time of trial; the spirit indeed is willing, but the flesh is weak" (Matthew 26:41). It is for ordinary people.

Biblical Wisdom

So I find it to be a law that when I want to do what is good, evil lies close at hand. For I delight in the law of God in my inmost self, but I see in my members another law at war with the law of my mind, making me captive to the law of sin that dwells in my members. Wretched man that I am! Who will rescue me from this body of death? Thanks be to God through Jesus Christ our Lord!

Romans 7:21-25

Theological Thoughts

Whoever prays the Lord's Prayer is not outstandingly pious, not a religious superstar; he does not ask God for opportunity to prove his faith, but asks not to be put to the test. He does not, of course, require that God take from him the great and onerous gift of freedom, but he does ask to be kept from those situations in which a wrong decision might almost force itself on him.[45]

Silence for Meditation

Questions to Ponder

- Do you agree that the Lord's Prayer is not for spiritual athletes? Explain.
- What is the relationship between asking for forgiveness and asking for protection from trials?
- With respect to trials, what are some of the ways in which we are not in control?

Psalm Fragment

Search me, O God, and know my heart;
test me and know my thoughts.
See if there is any wicked way in me,
and lead me in the way everlasting.
Psalm 139:23-24

Journal Reflections

- Which of the two individuals in Jesus' story do you most identify with? Why?
- Write about a time when you had to admit that you were not in control when faced with a temptation or trial?
- When he felt out of control, Paul asked who could save him. He answered, *"Thanks be to God through Jesus Christ our Lord!"* Does his answer work for you? Why or why not?

Prayer for Today

Thanks be to God through Jesus Christ our Lord! Amen.

Journey
Day 34—Saturday

Save us from the time of trial . . .

In the wilderness, Jesus confronted the temptations that are common to human-kind (Matthew 4:1-10). A hungry Jesus was tempted to turn stone into bread, a metaphor for the temptation to make material comfort one's highest value. It is the temptation to live by the values and practices of our materialistic, consumerist society, values and practices we hardly question because they are so widely accepted.

Those who succumb to this temptation live by the maxim that "the one who dies with the most toys wins." To Jesus' mind, the one who dies with the most toys loses: "What does it profit them if they gain the whole world, but lose or forfeit themselves?" (Luke 9:25). When we pray to be saved from the time of trial we are asking for the grace to say, "No! No more! Enough is enough."

Jesus was tempted by power. The tempter offered him "all the kingdoms of the world and their splendor" (a metaphor for political, economic, military, and personal power over others), but he would have to end his relationship with God and worship and serve evil. Jesus said no to this temptation. When we pray to be saved from the time of trial, we are praying for the grace to resist the lure of power and to embrace the humility that serves (Mark 10:42-45).

Vulnerable and at risk in the wilderness, Jesus was also tempted to test rather than trust God. This is an insidious temptation. The temptation for Jesus was in the suggestion that "*if* you are the son of God then bad things shouldn't happen to you, should they?" The temptation for us is the same: "*If* I am a child of God, bad things shouldn't happen to me, should they? So why do I have cancer; why did I lose my job; why did my marriage break up; why does my child take drugs; why is my house being foreclosed? So, God, do something to prove to me that I am your child, do something to make it right." Jesus said no to this temptation; rather than test God's love, he entrusted himself to God's love. When we pray to be saved from the time of trial, we are praying that no experiences, no circumstances, no disappointments would come between us and God. We are praying for the grace to entrust ourselves to God's love.

Biblical Wisdom

For we do not have a high priest who is unable to sympathize with our weaknesses, but we have one who in every respect has been tested as we are, yet without sin. Let us therefore approach the throne of grace with boldness, so that we may receive mercy and find grace to help in time of need.

Hebrews 4:15-16

Theological Thoughts

Lead us not into temptation is the opposite of any ecstatic boast of spiritual renewal, and enthusiastic cry for a chance to prove one's power over evil. It is full of realism about the vulnerability of the disciple, in spite of the inbreaking of the new world, in spite of membership in the new community.[46]

Silence for Meditation

Questions to Ponder

- Does it matter that Jesus has "in every respect" been tested as we are? Why or why not?
- In what ways might a church be tempted by "bread," power, and the desire to test God?
- In what ways (and why) does conventional culture suggest that giving in to these temptations is a good thing?

Psalm Fragment
Our soul waits for the LORD;
he is our help and shield.
Our heart is glad in him,
because we trust in his holy name.
Psalm 33:20-21

Journal Reflections

- Make a list of ways you are tempted by bread. Give it to God and pray for protection.

- Make a list of ways you are tempted by power. Give it to God and pray for protection.
- Make a list of ways you are tempted to test God. Give it to God and pray for protection.

Worship Hints for Tomorrow

- What trials or temptations distract you from worship? Ask God for protection and help.
- Before worship look at the altar and say, "God be merciful to me," with a smile on your face.

Prayer for Today

Gracious God, today I will do my best to entrust myself to your love and look for signs of your presence in the situations and circumstances of my life. Amen.

Journey
Day 35—Monday

Save us from the time of trial

Although it may seem strange to us, one trial Jesus' earliest followers would have prayed to be saved from was that of the apocalyptic cataclysm that was expected to bring terror to the earth before God would finally cause God's kingdom to come and God's will to be done on earth.

Once, Jesus' disciples asked him about the circumstances that would surround the coming of the kingdom:

> "Teacher, when will this be, and what will be the sign that this is about to take place?" And he said . . . "When you hear of wars and insurrections, do not be terrified; for these things must take place first, but the end will not follow immediately." Then he said to them, "Nation will rise against nation, and kingdom against kingdom; there will be great earthquakes, and in various places famines

Could the sign be - Isaiah 42:4 - He will not grow faint & be crushed until he has established justice to the earth

and plagues; and there will be dreadful portents and great signs from heaven."
(Luke 21:7ff.; cf. Mark 13:1ff.; and Matthew 24:3ff.)

Despite the popularity of the Left Behind series of novels, most American Christians do not spend much time worrying about end-of-time catastrophes and the imminent destruction of the world. Nevertheless, Jesus' words ring a bell with us—they sadly describe the world we live in. Think terrorism, think insurgencies all over the globe, think 9/11 and airplanes flown as bombs into buildings, think suicide bombers. Think about wars in the Middle East, in Caucasia, in Africa, rumors of war in the Balkans. Think genocide. Think tsunami, typhoon and hurricane and tornado, earthquake and fire. Think HIV/AIDS. Think global warming and climate change. Think about great and terrible events, both natural and human made, seemingly beyond our control, that threaten to overwhelm us, to turn our world upside down, to plunge us into fear and suffering and sorrow.

Imagine the trials faced by the people of Darfur, of Israel and Palestine, of Iraq. Imagine the trials faced by the people in Bangladesh and Burma, in Indonesia and China, in New Orleans and Florida, Kansas and Missouri, and all along a flooding Mississippi River. Imagine the trials of people suddenly stricken with life-threatening disease and no health care, of people whose homes have been foreclosed, whose jobs have been lost, who can't pay their bills.

When we pray to be saved from the time of trial, we are praying for ourselves and for all others to be saved from just such trials—and we are praying for the grace to stand with those to whom such trials sadly come.

Biblical Wisdom
I consider that the sufferings of this present time are not worth comparing with the glory about to be revealed to us. For the creation waits with eager longing for the revealing of the children of God.
   Romans 8:18-19

Theological Thoughts
Here at the end of the prayer a yearning makes itself heard, a yearning for that world in which [the evil] affecting our entire life will vanish.[47]

Silence for Meditation

Questions to Ponder

- With so many suffering from natural disasters and human evil, why pray to be saved from the time of trial?
- Is it important for a Christian to believe the biblical prophecies of end-time terror and tribulation? Why or why not?
- How does your church respond to people suffering from natural or human-caused trials?

Psalm Fragment

Truly the eye of the LORD is on those who fear him,
*   on those who hope in his steadfast love,*
to deliver their soul from death,
*   and to keep them alive in famine.*
    Psalm 33:18-19

Journal Reflections

- Have you ever suffered from a time of trial? If so, where was God in your experience?
- In what ways did other people of faith support you in your time of trial?
- In what ways have you been present to other people when they were in a time of trial?

Prayer for Today

Loving God, open my eyes to see your compassion in the love and support of people around me. Amen.

Psalm 36;11 - Do not let the foot of the
arrogant tread on me,
    or the hand of the wicked drive
        me away.
36:10 - O continue your steadfast love
        to those that know you.
    and your salvation to
        to the upright heart

Journey
Day 36—Tuesday

Save us from the time of trial...

Although it doesn't happen much in the United States, there are many places in the world where people of Christian faith suffer great trials simply because they are people of Christian faith. When you stand with God, it stands to reason that those who stand against God will stand against you as well.

Such was Jesus' experience. His faithfulness to God's will led to his humiliating and agonizing death on a Roman cross. It was not what he wanted. In the Garden of Gethsemane the night before he was killed, he prayed with great anguish to be spared such a death—but he ended his prayer by saying, "Yet, not my will but yours be done" (Luke 22:42).

When he had finished praying, Jesus returned to his disciples and found them asleep. He woke them and asked, "Why are you sleeping? Get up and pray that you may not come into the time of trial" (Luke 22:46). It is the prayer of people who choose to follow Jesus in the way of God, knowing that it could get them into trouble with those who don't.

Jesus was clear about what it meant to follow him: "If any want to become my followers, let them deny themselves and take up their cross daily and follow me." No one can predict where taking up the cross and following Jesus will take us. We can predict, however, that if Jesus was hated for who and how he was, there is a good chance people won't like who and how we are either—if we live our faith (John 15:18). And so we pray, "Save us from the time of trial."

It is important to note that Christians are not masochists—we don't seek to suffer for our faith and we know that there is no particular merit in suffering for our faith. But Christians are realists who understand that, in a violent world, faithfulness to the Prince of Peace may well lead to persecution, to testing, to the time of trial. We take the risks inherent in faithfulness with the same confidence Paul had when he wrote that nothing in all creation "will be able to separate us from the love of God in Christ Jesus our Lord" (Romans 8:39).

When we pray to be saved from the time of trial, we pray that our faith would not be tested, but if it is, we pray that God would be with us throughout and beyond the trial.

Biblical Wisdom
Because he himself was tested by what he suffered, he is able to help those who are being tested.
    Hebrews 2:18

Theological Thoughts
In praying to God to deliver us we acknowledge that God is greater than any foe of God. The power of evil must be admitted and taken seriously, yet not too seriously.[48]

Silence for Meditation

Questions to Ponder
· Given how Jesus was treated, what conclusions might we draw from the fact that the church and Christians are so often treated with ridicule or indifference in our culture?
· How is Jesus able to help those whose faith is being tested?
· Why do you think that in parts of the world where the church and Christians are persecuted, the church grows more rapidly than in places where there is no persecution?

Psalm Fragment
Even though I walk through the darkest valley,
        I fear no evil;
for you are with me;
        your rod and your staff—
        they comfort me.
    Psalm 23:4

Journal Reflections

- Have you ever suffered because you are a person of Christian faith? If so, describe the experience. What helped you stay faithful?
- Do you have a spiritual friend for mutual support? If so, write about the friendship and how it supports you in living your faith. If not, why not try to get such a friend?
- Write a short poem that expresses your confidence in God's presence in times of trouble.

Prayer for Today

Loving God, you are not ashamed of me; may I not be ashamed to show others my faith. Amen.

Prayer of the day (ELBW)
... that we may not fail you or deny
you in the time of trial ...

Psalm 71 -

V 9 - Do not cast me off in ~~old age~~
the time of old age
do not forsake me when my
strength is spent

V 2a - In your righteousness deliver
me and rescue me

Journey Week Seven

Days 37–38

And deliver us from evil.

Day 39

For the kingdom, the power, and the glory are yours, now and forever.

Day 40

Amen.

Journey
Day 37—Wednesday

And deliver us from evil.

When Jesus taught this prayer, his followers would have had no trouble accepting the idea of evil personified in the devil and his legions of demons. The Greek word that translates into English as *evil* can also be translated "the evil one." In the minds of Jesus' followers, prayer to be delivered from the "evil one" would have made perfect sense.

The writer of Ephesians expressed a commonly held belief when he declared, "For our struggle is not against enemies of blood and flesh, but against the rulers, against the authorities, against the cosmic powers of this present darkness, against the spiritual forces of evil in the heavenly places" (Ephesians 6:12).

In our day and age, we may be less inclined to personify evil, but there are very few who would deny the existence of evil. The evidence is too overwhelming. We may not see the "powers of this present darkness" as demonic beings, but we know that there are indeed powers that rage against the rule of God, powers that seem to take "possession" of us and place us in conflict with the will of God—even those of us who pray for the will of God to be done!

Racism, sexism, ageism, classism, nationalism, homophobia, xenophobia—every form of discrimination, bigotry, prejudice, hatred—are among the suprapersonal powers of evil that turn God's good creation into a human wasteland of unnecessary suffering. The powers that rage against the rule and will of God build dividing walls that separate individuals, groups, communities, nations. Those who pray to be delivered from evil pray for the grace to say "No!" to walls that divide, knowing that Christ is about the breaking down of any and all dividing walls (Ephesians 2:14). As Paul declared, "There is no longer Jew or Greek, there is no longer slave or free, there is no longer male and female; for all of you are one in Christ Jesus" (Galatians 3:28).

When we pray to be delivered from evil, we pray for the grace to "not be overcome by evil" and the grace to "overcome evil with good" (Romans 12:21). In other words, for the grace to follow Jesus in the way of God.

Biblical Wisdom
The Lord will rescue me from every evil attack and save me for his heav-
enly kingdom. To him be the glory forever and ever. Amen.
    2 Timothy 4:18

Theological Thoughts
In the act of praying this prayer, devils are loosed. The "powers that be" rage
against such prayer, can't stand to have one free person running loose who is able
to throw off the chains and pray, "Our Father . . . save us."[49]

Silence for Meditation

Questions to Ponder
· How would you define evil?
· What evidence do you see that evil is a supra-personal force and not just the
  acts of individuals?
· Do you agree that bad institutions can make good people do bad things?
  Why or why not?

Psalm Fragment
God is our refuge and strength,
        a very present help in trouble.
    Psalm 46:1

Journal Reflections
· Have you ever had an experience that felt like an experience of real evil? If so,
  describe the experience and how it affected you.
· How do you explain the existence of evil in a world where God created everything that is?
· In what ways does the belief that Christ has defeated "sin, death, and the
  devil" influence your attitude toward evil?

Prayer for Today

God, no matter what happens to me today, let me remember that I am baptized and belong to you. Amen.

Journey
Day 38—Holy Thursday

And deliver us from evil.

In our plea to be delivered from evil we return to the first three petitions—our prayer for God's name to be made holy, for God's kingdom to come, for God's will to be done on earth as in heaven. When those petitions have been finally and fully answered, we will have been delivered from evil. So there is in this last petition a hint of longing, the longing that things will finally come out all right for the world God loves. There is a yearning for God to put things right, to replace human sorrow with joy, human tears with laughter, human fear with peace.

The vision of John on the island of Patmos in many ways sums up what we who pray the Lord's Prayer long for:

Then I saw a new heaven and a new earth; for the first heaven and the first earth had passed away. . . . And I heard a loud voice from the throne saying,
"See, the home of God is among mortals.
He will dwell with them as their God;
they will be his peoples,
and God himself will be with them;
he will wipe every tear from their eyes.
Death will be no more;
mourning and crying and pain will be no more,
for the first things have passed away."
And the one who was seated on the throne said, "See, I am making all things new." Also he said, "Write this, for these words are trustworthy and true." Then

he said to me, "It is done! I am the Alpha and the Omega, the beginning and the end. To the thirsty I will give water as a gift from the spring of the water of life." (Revelation 21:1-6)

It is a profound vision, and we who live between the vision and the coming true of the vision have the prayer Jesus taught us as a roadmap for the journey.

Biblical Wisdom
Rejoice in the Lord always; again I will say, Rejoice. Let your gentleness be known to everyone. The Lord is near. Do not worry about anything, but in everything by prayer and supplication with thanksgiving let your requests be made known to God. And the peace of God, which surpasses all understanding, will guard your hearts and your minds in Christ Jesus.
Philippians 4:4-7

Theological Thoughts
The final petition brings the prayer full circle. It identifies the inescapable paradox within which those who pray this prayer live. Luther captured this paradox in his famous *simul justus et peccator*, the paradox of being simultaneously a righteous person and a sinner.[50]

Silence for Meditation

Questions to Ponder
- Why do vision and poetry, music and art often express spiritual truth better than a sermon?
- In what ways is human creativity a powerful and appropriate response to evil?
- In what ways might worship be seen as a "divine drama"?

Psalm Fragment
My soul clings to you;
   your right hand upholds me.
Psalm 63:8

Journal Reflections

- In your religious imagination, how important is the idea of the full coming of God's kingdom?
- Write a poem or hymn lyric, or draw or paint a picture, or compose some music that expresses a moment of spiritual joy.
- In what ways do you experience yourself as, at the same time, both saint and sinner?

Prayer for Today

Creator God, you are light and in you there is not darkness at all; of what shall I be afraid? Amen.

Journey
Day 39—Good Friday

For the kingdom, the power, and the glory are yours, now and forever.

The oldest manuscripts of Matthew and Luke do not have these words at the end of the Lord's Prayer. It seems they were probably added by the church at a later date.

This little addition to the Lord's Prayer makes it "our" prayer, the church's prayer. Jesus has taught us to pray, and the church's doxology (words of praise) signals that we have learned our lesson well: it is "your name," not my name; "your kingdom," not my kingdom; "your will," not my will—*"For the kingdom, the power, and the glory are yours, now and forever."*

It was a seditious thing to say in the first century. It is a seditious thing to say in the twenty-first century. There are many who arrogantly claim the kingdom, the power, and the glory belong to them—and them alone. By tacking this little doxology on to the end of the prayer that Jesus taught them, the church was putting the world on notice that Caesar is not Lord—God is Lord. Whether Caesar lives in Rome or Washington, D.C., in Moscow or London, in Beijing or New Delhi or Paris, Caesar is not Lord, God is Lord.

First-century Christians let the "powers that be" know where their allegiances lay every time they prayed this prayer. They lived under the rule of God, not the rule of Caesar. When the rule of Caesar and the rule of God did not conflict, there was no problem. When the rule of God and the rule of Caesar did conflict, they lived under the rule of God.

When we pray this prayer and end it with the church's doxology, we remind ourselves and others where *our* allegiances lie. Christians should not make good nationalists—they are citizens of a kingdom whose moral boundaries completely transcend the geopolitical boundaries where Caesar falsely claims the kingdom, the power, and the glory.

It is a radical claim and it has gotten uncounted followers of Jesus into trouble with Caesar for more than 2,000 years now. It is a claim we are bold to make: "Now to him who is able to keep you from falling, and to make you stand without blemish in the presence of his glory with rejoicing, to the only God our Savior, through Jesus Christ our Lord, be glory, majesty, power, and authority, before all time and now and forever. Amen" (Jude 1:24-25).

Biblical Wisdom
And the Word became flesh and lived among us, and we have seen his glory, the glory as of a father's only son, full of grace and truth.
    John 1:14

Theological Thoughts
The kingdom, the power, and the glory, three large words are piled upon one another here, as the prayer ends, in one final shout of praise to God. Perhaps this prayer ought to be sung, as the church has done in various ways, rather than said.[51]

Silence for Meditation

Questions to Ponder
- What is "glory"?
- Was it appropriate for the church to add these lines to Jesus' prayer? Why or why not?

- Is it seditious to declare that the kingdom, the power, and the glory are God's? Explain.

Psalm Fragment
Be exalted, O God, above the heavens.
   Let your glory be over all the earth.
   Psalm 57:5

Journal Reflections
- Write a short meditation titled "Where My Allegiances Lie."
- In what ways might being a Christian be countercultural?
- How does your life express that the kingdom, the power, and the glory belong to God?

Prayer for Today
Let my life show that the power and the kingdom and the glory are yours alone. Amen.

Journey
Day 40—Saturday

Amen.

We come to the end of our Lenten journey with a resounding "Amen!" This little word affirms that this is our prayer. *Amen* is a Hebrew word that carries the meaning of certainly, verily, truthfully. When it follows a prayer or hymn of praise, this little word indicates the assent and desire of the one who prays. It could be translated as a confident "So be it!"

So be it—God's name shall be made holy, God's kingdom shall come, God's will shall be done on earth as it is in heaven. So be it—God does and shall continue to provide "daily bread," God does and shall continue to draw us into a circle of forgiveness where we forgive as we have already been forgiven. So be it—God stands with us in times of trial and when faced with evil. The kingdom and power and glory are God's alone, forever. Amen! So be it!

The central words in this prayer—*Father, name, kingdom, will, bread, forgive, trial, evil*—are shorthand, symbols that convey worlds of meaning for people of Christian faith. We have played around the edges of these meanings for forty days, but we have not by any means plumbed their depths. That is the work of a lifetime of prayer and meditation, reading and study, and living faithfully in the places and relationships where we spend our lives.

I suggest that you begin and end each day with the Lord's Prayer. If you live alone, let it be your first words upon awakening and your last words before sleeping. If you have a spouse, begin and end the day praying this prayer together. If you have children, begin and end the day as a family with this prayer. And then throughout the day—in the situations and circumstances of your daily life—mediate on one petition each day (there are seven—one for each day of the week). You might begin with "Our Father in heaven, hallowed be your name" on Sunday, then move on to "your kingdom come" on Monday, and so on. Daily examine the events and relationships of your life in the light of this prayer. In this way, your life *becomes* prayer.

Biblical Wisdom
Now to him who by the power at work within us is able to accomplish abundantly far more than all we can ask or imagine, to him be glory in the church and in Christ Jesus to all generations, forever and ever. Amen.
Ephesians 3:20-21

Theological Thoughts
"Amen, amen" means "Yes, yes, it is going to come about just like this."[52]

Silence for Meditation

Questions to Ponder
- In what ways is the Lord's Prayer a summary of Jesus' teaching?
- How can the Lord's Prayer guide the mission of the church?

- How can the Lord's Prayer serve as a lens through which we critically view our society?

Psalm Fragment

Deliverance belongs to the LORD;

may your blessing be on your people!

Psalm 3:8

Journal Reflections

- In what ways has your understanding of the Lord's Prayer changed in these forty days?
- Will your life of faith be any different for having made this journey with the Lord's Prayer? If so, how?
- In what ways (if any) has this journey with the Lord's Prayer changed the way you think about and participate in your faith community?

Worship Hints for Tomorrow

- Put some oomph into your voice when you pray the doxology at the end of the Lord's Prayer.
- After worship, give a copy of this book to someone else in your faith community and encourage them to take the journey.

Prayer for Today

Jesus, as I finish this book on the prayer you taught us to pray, I know that my journey continues and you are my constant traveling companion. Thank you. Amen. Amen. Amen.

Notes

1   *Opening the Book of Faith: Lutheran Insights for Bible Study* (Minneapolis: Augsburg Fortress, 2008). All of the essays in this book are well worth reading. In "God's Powerful Book," the Rev. Stanley Olson shows the place of the Bible in the life and faith of the church and individual Christians. In "How Can the Bible Be Studied," Diane Jacobson introduces several important ways Christians enter into conversation with God's Word.

2   Ibid., 29.

3   Ibid., 33.

4   See Diane Jacobson's essay in *Opening the Book of Faith: Lutheran Insights for Bible Study* (Minneapolis: Augsburg Fortress, 2008) for a fuller introduction to the different ways of reading the Bible.

5   These hints for journaling come from my friend, Ron Klug, whose book *How to Keep a Spiritual Journal* (Minneapolis: Augsburg Books, 1993) is an excellent guide to spiritual journaling.

6   Leonardo Boff, *The Lord's Prayer: The Prayer of Integral Liberation*, trans. Theodore Morrow (New York: Orbis, 1983), 5, 20.

7   Daniel L. Migliore, preface to *The Lord's Prayer: Perspectives for Reclaiming Christian Prayer*, ed. Daniel L. Migliore (Grand Rapids: Eerdmans, 1993), 1-2.

8   Hans Dieter Betz, *The Sermon on the Mount* (Minneapolis: Fortress Press, 1995), 388.

9   Eduard Schweizer, *The Good News According to Matthew* (Atlanta: John Knox, 1975), 150.

10 Martin Luther, "The Small Catechism," in *The Book of Concord*, ed. Robert Kolb and Timothy Wengert (Minneapolis: Fortress Press, 2000), 356.

11 Amy-Jill Levine, *The Misunderstood Jew* (San Francisco: HarperSanFrancisco, 2006), 42.

12 The Greek word *baseleia*, which is usually translated with the somewhat static noun "kingdom" in English Bibles, can also have the more dynamic meaning of "reign" or "rule." It seems clear in the Gospels that Jesus usually had the dynamic meaning in mind when he used the word; he invited people to live purposefully under the rule or reign of God in the here and now.

13 The Greek word can be translated as either "among" or "within," and different Bible translations choose differently. I suspect that both meanings were intended and should be held in tension with each other for the fullest meaning of this text.

14 Luther, "The Small Catechism," 356.

15 John Koenig, *Rediscovering New Testament Prayer* (Harrisburg: Morehouse, 1992), 47.

16 William Willimon and Stanley Hauerwas, *Lord Teach Us: The Lord's Prayer & the Christian Life* (Nashville: Abingdon, 1996), 50.

17 Martin Luther, *A Treatise on Christian Liberty*, trans. W. A. Lambert (Philadelphia: Fortress Press, 1957), 34.

18 Willimon and Hauerwas, 51.

19 Koenig, 45.

20 Oscar Cullman, *Prayer in the New Testament* (Minneapolis: Fortress Press, 1995), 46.

21 Luther, "The Small Catechism," 357.

22 If you are interested in the topic of "affluenza," please see: John de Graaf, David Wann, Thomas Naylor, *Affluenza: The All-Consuming Epidemic* (San

Francisco: Berrett-Koehler, 2005), and/or Clive Hamilton, Richard Denniss, *Affluenza: When Too Much Is Never Enough* (Sydney: Allen and Unwin, 2006).

23 Willimon and Hauerwas, 64.

24 Ibid., 66.

25 Schweizer, 153.

26 Mother Teresa Quotes, http://home.att.net/~hillcrestbaptist/mt.html.

27 Willimon and Hauerwas, 69.

28 Betz, 392.

29 John Donne, "Meditation 17," 1624.

30 Betz, 400.

31 Luther, "The Small Catechism," 357.

32 Robert Smith, *Matthew*, Augsburg Commentary on the New Testament (Minneapolis: Augsburg, 1989), 112.

33 N. T. Wright, *The Lord and His Prayer* (Grand Rapids: Eerdmans, 1996), 36.

34 Saint Augustine, *Confessions* (Grand Rapids: Sovereign Grace, 1971), 1.

35 Smith, 112.

36 Willimon and Hauerwas, 73.

37 Luther, "The Small Catechism," 358.

38 Henry French, "A Primer on Mission in the Way of Jesus," *Word and World*, Winter 2002: 25.

39 Willimon and Hauerwas, 84.

40 Smith, 113.

41 Schweizer, 155.

42 Smith, 113.

43 Luther, "The Small Catechism," 358.

44 Craig S. Keener, *A Commentary on the Gospel of Matthew* (Grand Rapids: Eerdmans, 1999), 225.

45 Schweizer, 156.

46 Smith, 113.

47 Schweizer, 156.

48 Willimon and Hauerwas, 94.

49 Ibid., 91.

50 French, 25.

51 Willimon and Hauerwas, 98.

52 Luther, "The Small Catechism," 358.